HAPPY SAMURAI

Happiness through Bushido
Training in the 21st Century

LUKE MAYES

D1518317

Cover design: Malcolm Steward, www.malcolmsteward.com

Calligraphy: Masami Morimoto, www. masami-morimoto.com

For Andi and Veronica

"Sometimes the warrior needs to be alone, meditate, and remind himself of who he is and who he wants to be."

—Dr. Bohdi Sanders

I dedicate this book with much love and respect to Grand Master Kaicho Nakamura

HAPPY SAMURAI

Contents

LUKE MAYES

Foreword

I met Kyoshi Luke Mayes when he started his training at World Seido Karate Headquarters in New York City in 1996. From the very first day, he approached his martial arts training with complete dedication, diligence, and sincerity – not only with regard to the physical aspects of the curriculum set forth for each level and rank, but more prevalently, with his uncompromising focus on his path toward his own personal growth and development – mentally, emotionally, and spiritually.

A devoted student, his skill as a practitioner and the manner in which he approaches his practice inspires those he trains alongside, many of whom he has developed great friendships with. He brings a great energy onto the training floor as well as into tournaments where he often excels at many of his events. While fearless as a competitor, he is even more greatly respected for his humor, gracious demeanor, and support of fellow competitors. He is admired as an instructor, most notably as part of our Children's program having joined our teaching staff soon after he began his own training at Seido. Always generous with his time and driven to always give back, he has taught a countless number of kids starting as young as four shepherding many throughout their training to achieve their black belts and even well into their teen years as they transitioned into our adult program.

His most profound contribution to the many young lives he has touched, however, reaches far beyond teaching them how to kick and punch. He has always made it his priority to instill in them the importance of appreciation and respect for their parents, family, teachers, friends, their community, and above all, to have confidence that they can reach and surpass any goals they set for themselves, to never give up when they face challenges—because they have the tools learned throughout their training, and with that, they always have everything they need within themselves to succeed. Always.

In these pages, you'll follow Kyoshi Luke along his own personal journey—his challenges, his motivations, his inspirations. Through many years of courageous introspection and honest reflection upon how his life has unfolded thus far—within framework of the lessons he has learned that have shaped his own bushido—you will get a glimpse of someone whose integrity permeates the path he has chosen to guide him. It is an honor to have been asked to write this foreword for one of our most dedicated students who continues to strive toward always learning and growing. This book is only one example of that and we very much look forward to seeing where his journey leads next. Enjoy.

Osu.

Nidaime A. Nakamura
Vice Chairman & Chief Instructor
World Seido Karate Honbu (Headquarters)
Seido Johshin Honzan, Westchester Dojo

LUKE MAYES

Author's Note

What better time than this present moment to conquer fear with love? What better time to curb anxiety with courage? What better time to quiet the panic in our hearts with self-control and magnanimity?

The eight tenets of the samurai have never been more poignant in my life than they are this very day, when the world faces a global pandemic. It's easy to discard noble notions as idealistic and out of reach. The truth, however, is that happiness can be nurtured and created through the reflection of these eight tenets, and the truth can be examined and assessed for what it really is, rather than what the imagined worst-case scenario might be. When the tornado comes and the wind blows, we must find shelter and take action. We should not manifest the fear provoked by the very thought of the tornado, though.

I wrote *Happy Samurai* to provide a resource for people to find more happiness in their life. The current climate presents a unique challenge to appreciate how this happiness can dramatically affect the quality of this thing called life. Happiness allows us to make better decisions in tough times with a clear head and a loving heart. The world right now, more than ever, needs happy samurai.

Righteousness (or justice) provides the grace to do the right thing, to give blood if we're healthy and deliver food or care to the elderly or anyone who is more vulnerable with a lowered immunity.

Courage allows us to stay strong, despite the bombardment of panic and chaos that surrounds us. Courage doesn't rid us of fear or doubt, but it allows us to manage the present moment so we can take care of those with less courage.

Benevolence encourages us to become useful in our society and step up when leadership is required and when kindness and compassion are desperately needed. We become less burdened and more eager to help.

Respect for the danger of this virus goes hand in hand with our respect for our fellow human beings. The opportunity to spend more time giving people our undivided attention has never been better.

Sincerity cuts through the clutter and gets to the very heart of the matter. We can skip the egocentric image and be our best and truest authentic self.

Honor commands us to look after our parents, our loved ones, the elderly in our community, and all who cannot fend for themselves.

Loyalty to our place in the various communities where we live creates an action plan that is fluid but present and makes decisions easier and more dynamic.

Self-control guides us to reexamine the other seven tenets and to live more in the moment. A commitment to meditation makes it exponentially easier to practice self-control.

This virus is no match for the happy samurai within us all.

Kyoshi Luke Mayes
Santa Barbara, California
March 2020

Introduction

I was a teenager in control of a multi-million-dollar piece of machinery that went really fast. I was in heaven.

While flying on a night sortie over RNZAF (Royal New Zealand Air Force) base Ohakea, I soaked up the tranquility of being alone in my Strikemaster jet. The stars shone above me, and the lights of Palmerston North twinkled below me. The red, dimly lit instrument panel ensured that I maintained my night vision, so I could see for miles. I always enjoyed night flying. I felt at peace and in control of the set-up as I was about to start my instrument approach. Then I felt it. In an instant, that heavenly peace was shattered.

I felt a developing vibration throughout the cockpit, and my heart rate kicked up a notch. That warm fuzzy feeling chilled to cold panic. I was flying low, so without the luxury of altitude to assess the situation. I called off the approach as I checked my instruments. I knew I could eject, if I needed to, but that was a last resort. I needed to think fast.

It's easy to panic in these moments of stress, and it's very hard to keep calm. The truth is, my inability to stay in the present moment could have cost me my life that night. What I also know is this was one of the many experiences that led me to write this book. In a bind, we resort to what we know. But it's also true that we know best what we've practiced. Practice can make perfect (or close to it), but in the end we become what we practice, day in, day out.

There's no doubt that the kind of training that installed me as a pilot behind the controls of my Strikemaster jet informed my flying expertise, but something else was responsible in a big way. It's what kept me behind those controls with the kind of peace and meditative calm that, time and again, have instinctively guided me.

It's what kept me from immediately, at the first sign of trouble, saying goodbye, bailing out, and simply allowing the aircraft to spiral and crash into the ground. It's also what can keep you grounded when things begin to hit a spiral.

A combination of my martial arts training and my military training helped me to address the panic and work through the problem that night, but we'll get to that later.

As a small, skinny, twelve-year-old boy among adult men and women, I recited the dojo kun at the start and finish of every karate class. There were police officers in my class. They weren't there to waste time. The atmosphere was always serious and often frightening. The very air was thick with sweat and bushido spirit. I felt protected and safe but never comfortable. The shared ethos of ordinary people prepared to sweat it out in their search for self-improvement touched my heart and continues to do so.

Four decades have come and gone, and the words we recited several times per week with military precision are stilled emblazoned in my brain:

"Hitotsu! Jinkaku kansei ni tsutomeru koto…"

No, I hadn't run away from home to join a cult, and this isn't an invitation to join one.

This book, in a nutshell, is a description of how that ancient bushido spirit has influenced me. An influence that, way back when, channeled my energy along a path and has instinctively, time and again, brought me back to Earth, literally and figuratively.

What does this have to do with what happened as my Strikemaster and I sliced through the night sky?

A lot, it turns out.

It's about courage and developing the confidence to face seemingly insurmountable challenges.

Life in itself is dotted with a never-ending array of challenges. If we develop the tools to embrace those challenges, we're effectively charting a path to happiness.

There's no magic bullet to happiness, because we'll be faced with challenges for the rest of our lives. That's why developing those tools is an ongoing, disciplined, daily process.

That's the process I found in that sweaty, intimidating space where I first learned karate. The time-tested tenets of the samurai are as effective today as they were more than 800 years ago.

I know because I've been rewarded many times over by traveling this path.

It may all seem like a contradiction, especially since falling back on what we know could be an obstacle to stepping into something new. One exception is when I stepped into something new more than forty years ago. That something "new" I stepped into never gets old. And even before I became a pilot in the RNZAF, it had already helped me build the warrior spirit to stick with it on that frightful night, so I could bring my Strikemaster safely back to Earth.

I was a Happy Samurai then, and will continue to be a Happy Samurai many times over, as I fall back on the way of the samurai (what I know) to face life's daily challenges.

This is what informed my determination to write this book in the hope that, in the chapters that follow, you'll be encouraged to harness the spirit of bushido in order to realize the lifelong, moment-to-moment victories that define a Happy Samurai.

Having studied martial arts for over forty years and having been married to (and divorced from) two amazing women, I have navigated a unique path to discover what bushido means in the twenty-first century. My aim is to give you the benefit of some of my experiences without your necessarily having to go through said experiences to obtain some of the lessons and (hopefully) wisdom that come as a result.

So, what is bushido? Bushido was fully developed in the sixteenth century and was influenced by Shinto and Zen Buddhism, so the violent nature of the samurai could be tempered and further developed with wisdom. The "warrior way" is not just for battle, but also for application in everyday life to tackle our own demons and to manage our best selves in the world that surrounds us.

I don't use the word "warrior" lightly. I give my heartfelt gratitude and respect to members of the military, police force, and fire department, and to all hospital staff who truly deal with life-and-death battles every day. I do not belittle the tremendous sacrifice these bastions of our community give us when I refer to a "warrior way" or a "Bushido" spirit in everyday civilian life. We can all take the example of these true "warriors" and find more purpose in what we do to become happy samurai with a non-quitting spirit of service to our community.

I grew up on the North Shore in Auckland, New Zealand. I joined Chidokan Karate-Do and studied under (now Shihan) Neil Parker Sensei. My mother was shocked when she came to watch a demonstration and my instructor lightly kicked the side of my face with a controlled roundhouse kick. What had I gotten myself into to?

We trained on the two days a week that the local dojo (located in the Pupuke Tennis Club) was open. I'd then travel across town to Avondale to train with (Kancho) Jack Sims Sensei on Thursday nights. I'd travel either to Henderson or Te Atatu on Friday nights to train at any Chidokan dojo that was open. I was a kid training with adults, and I loved it. I travelled all over the city with another kid, Wayne Smith. Wayne's mum literally taxied us everywhere and anywhere to do karate. We were happy samurai.

The dojo kun (ethos/way of life) of Chidokan Karate-Do had a significant impact on my view of the world. We would recite the dojo kun in both English and Japanese. The words have been ingrained into my psyche. Repetition is a big part of martial arts training, and most of us need that so stuff eventually sticks. It can feel didactic at times, but it's a process. I will repeat many principles throughout this book; this is done with good reason.

The five precepts of the Chidokan dojo kun all start with the word "Hitotsu" which means "one" or "first." The use of the word "Hitotsu" is to underline that each is equally important.

1. To strive for the perfection of character.
2. To defend the paths of truth.
3. To honor the principles of etiquette.
4. To foster the spirit of effort.
5. To guard against impetuous courage.

These five guiding principles/ethics evolved from the Shotokan Karate dojo kun and generally credited to Master Gichin Funakoshi.

I started my Seido Karate-Do training in 1996 at Honbu dojo in New York City under Kaicho Nakamura. The access to Kaicho's martial arts lineage was not lost on me. A samurai descendant, Kaicho Nakamura was a student of Master Masutatsu Oyama, who himself was a student of Gichin Funakoshi.

I vividly remember meeting Kaicho for the first time. His every movement had purpose, and his eyes absorbed the room. His silent demeanor spoke volumes about his calm and steady focus. He introduced himself to me, and I felt like there was nothing else going on in the world. I had his undivided attention. He saw me. I was humbled. I was so in awe of his magnanimous presence that I knew I would be his student for life. I knew there was no need to talk about my previous karate experience, because it wasn't important in relation to what I needed to learn.

Bushido spirit (or "Budo" when applied to martial arts in general) can be trained and fostered, but I believe it is inherent in all of us. We are born with instincts and a drive that have been finely tuned over hundreds of thousands of years of evolution.

We are all born to be a happy samurai. As we grow and take on roles and responsibilities, we acquire personality traits and habits that take us away from the happy samurai we were born to be. The samurai tenets ask us to examine our own motives and question what is at the core of our personal set of values. Are we living true to the very best person we were born to be? If not, why not?

Like the Shotokan and Chidokan dojo kun, I want you to consider the eight tenets of the samurai as things to examine. It's not a step-by-step process. One is not necessarily more important than the other. Each has its merits and can be applied singularly or collectively. There's no right way or wrong way. It's your way, your "Do," that these tenets will help you to define better.

Let's take a look at the tenets of the samurai:

- ✴ Righteousness
- ✴ Courage
- ✴ Benevolence
- ✴ Respect
- ✴ Sincerity
- ✴ Honor
- ✴ Loyalty
- ✴ Self-Control

When listed, these eight tenets can be daunting and easily discarded as "idealistic" or "unattainable in the modern world," but I disagree!

The million-dollar question is: Can we live by these tenets with a sense of humor and adventure?

I believe we all can, and, most importantly, I believe you can, too.

What I offer is an examination of each of these tenets and a methodology in thinking, to achieve a life of more meaning and purpose. Your mission will become clearer and your sense of personal pride (not to be confused with ego) will grow stronger as a result, day by day.

I'm not offering solutions to achieve a "perfect" life. I'm offering an appreciation for a tried and tested mindset that will create a more meaningful life... little by little. You can adopt any or all of these bushido concepts and become a happier samurai as a result.

To follow the example of the dojo kun, I have titled each of the next eight chapters of this book starting with the number "1," to reinforce the idea that all are worth looking at and studying, individually or collectively.

     1: Righteousness (or Justice)

     1: Courage

     1: Benevolence (or Compassion)

     1: Respect

     1: Sincerity

     1: Honor

     1: Loyalty

     1: Self-Control

You do not need to be a martial artist to gain happiness through the tenets of the samurai. As Kaicho often says, "It's not just kicking and punching." Happiness is derived from so much more than kicks and punches.

1: Righteousness (or Justice)

"You should not deviate from the path of righteousness.
You should lead a life worthy of man."

—Bujinkan Grandmaster Dr. Masaaki Hatsumi Soke

If the ejection didn't compress my spine, the ballistically spread parachute could dislocate one or both of my hips. These thoughts were spinning through my head as the vibrations throughout my Strikemaster stabilized but didn't go away.

I was sitting on a live Martin-Baker Mk PB4 ejector seat. Even at low altitude, you were blown out of the canopy before a drogue gun in the seat fired a metal slug that deployed a small parachute, and the parachute would blast open. At the officer's mess, I'd learned that the Martin-Baker company sent you a tie, if you successfully ejected using one of their seats. Of all the approaches used to finish a sortie, ejection was jokingly called the, "Martin-Baker Let Down Approach."

All this noise in my head was needless (and useless) ejection-related trivia at a time when I had far more important and pressing matters to address. I was contemplating the repercussions of ejecting before I'd really started to look at the situation in the present moment.

I then realized I needed to check that I'd switched off the hydraulically operated spoiler/airbrake surfaces above the wings. I hadn't. My mistake. I'd done a touch-and-go landing at Palmerston and forgotten to disengage my airbrakes.

I switched the airbrakes off. The vibrating stopped, and I resumed my instrument approach, but I knew I'd over-sped the airbrakes and would need to report that to the maintenance crew. I knew the Wing Commander would find out about my mistake, as well. I wasn't going to get a Martin-Baker tie, but I was about to look stupid in front of my ground crew, my peers, and my commanding officer. I had some decisions to make…

Growing up in New Zealand, I was fascinated with martial arts from my early childhood. I used to go "ninja-ing" with my friend, Anthony, when I was ten years old. We would get dressed up as ninjas (all black or camo) and go to the local golf course, where we'd climb up trees and observe local golfers while hidden in the treetops. We didn't stalk people or steal things or vandalize anything. We were practicing the art of camouflage and observation. We were happy samurai. Our parents thought we were crazy!

I'm not saying my childhood was filled with only such honorable activities, but the motivation behind "ninja-ing" was a love for kung fu movies and the art of hide-and-seek. The intention was pure, and we shared a wonderful comradery with a small group of friends, who joined us from time to time as we "ninja-ed" throughout the neighborhood and threw shuriken at a large gum tree in my back yard, before disappearing into the local vegetation.

Righteousness doesn't define a particular belief system that has rules and regulations. Righteousness is what we feel in our gut. Righteousness is based on what we were born knowing to be right, before we were introduced and influenced by racism, fanaticism, dogma, or any number of societal pressures. We know that stealing is wrong, regardless of our religious beliefs or convictions. We know we should assist an elderly person to cross the street, regardless of whether we're a Republican or a Democrat. The key here is service to others. Righteousness at its very core means having the perspective to know instinctively what is right.

My "ninja-ing" friend, Anthony, and I went to Rosmini College with another bushido, Professor John Danaher (of Renzo Gracie BJJ fame). Our school motto was, "Legis Charitas Plenitudo," which translates to, "Charity Fulfills the Law." In essence, if we do what is right through giving to others, there is very little (if any) need for law(s). The three of us have all taken completely different paths in our martial arts journey, but we have all dedicated ourselves to teaching and giving service to our students.

If you choose to commit to providing service to others every day, your life will become infinitely richer and more meaningful.

Anthony went on to study ninjutsu under Dr. Masaaki Hatsumi (quoted at the start of this chapter) in Japan for over twenty-five years. Anthony "Tatsuji" Netzler became one of the first MMA fighters, before the sport became a worldwide phenomenon; he now teaches at his dojo in Mt. Maunganui in New Zealand.

(Shihan) Anthony's mission is to "train, teach, and help people study the art of Bujinkan Ninjutsu."

(Professor) John Danaher trains and teaches world-class MMA fighters at the Renzo Gracie dojo in New York City. He is an encyclopedia of jiu-jitsu knowledge and philosophy, and he teaches with an extraordinary sense of humor and passion for the sport.

(Professor) John Danaher sums up his philosophy perfectly when he says, "Learning how to learn is absolutely one of the keys to success in life in general and jiu-jitsu in particular."

The righteous virtue of these instructors is based on the intention behind what they chose to do with their lives. They are teachers at heart and want to pass on information and instruct students, so they can become better at the art but also can become more developed humans. That is the human side of bushido and what I believe is most important about the practice of martial arts in the twenty-first century. Students should be able to apply the art to defend themselves on the street or improve their fighting skills in the dojo, but without human development, it is a limited education.

Through the practice of teaching, I have discovered that I learn to teach better as I observe what works from student to student. The lessons we need to learn most are the lessons we teach best. Service to others is service to our best self and develops the happy samurai within.

Righteousness, justice, or virtue is our ability to maintain high moral standards. It is the ability to manage our own mind, something I will discuss in more detail in the chapter covering *Self-Control*. Righteousness is not about our ability to be perfect! We strive for the perfection of character, but it's a constant journey. Bushido training is about the path or way—rather than the destination. The process is the way, not the result.

To address righteousness directly, let's look at the seven deadly sins and examine how we combat these with a bushido spirit. To acknowledge that we are all susceptible to these universal "sins" is to learn to deal with that dark part of our nature. It is not a battle we win. It is a battle we fight every day. That is why martial arts training strengthens our mind, body, and spirit. We wake up each day undefeated, but ready for battle once again.

The seven deadly sins:

Lust

A Catholic boy's school is a place where male hormones abound. As school boys, we were told by the priests that "interfering" with ourselves was sinful and wrong. I'd spend half my life agonizing over this predicament and the rest of the time feeling guilty. From time to time, we'd see girls from our sister school, but we didn't talk much with them, because we were all so clueless about girls. Our only education on the female anatomy was a small collection of *Playboy* magazines that got circulated around. Lust was a daily battle.

At the very core of our animal self is the desire to reproduce, to keep the species alive. We have evolved to have sensations that drive us toward reproduction. This is a very natural state of being. As we grow older, that natural drive and those sensations morph into a complex battle with our desire for pleasure. While there is nothing wrong with pleasure, it becomes harmful when the desire or lust for pleasure overwhelms our ability to be happy without it.

Whether it be sex, drugs, alcohol, cigarettes, food, porn, money, power, or any number of desires that overwhelm us, martial arts training teaches us to stay strong and subdue these desires, if they create imbalance in our lives. Kaicho often says, "Cho Shin, Cho Soku, Cho Shin," which translates to, "Control your body, control your breathing, control your mind."

In moderation, any of the things we sometimes lust for can be part of a normal, healthy life, but the focus here is on staying in harmony with our best self. When we control our body, we send a message to our brain to hold or find a position. This is as relevant in meditation as it is in fighting. It is hard (if not impossible) to best control our breathing and our mind without first controlling our body. In practical application, if you feel yourself getting drawn into a lust for something that is not in harmony with your best self, stop. Stop where you are, and control the body.

Once the body is in a position you've determined, you can control your breathing. If possible, sit in an upright posture with your back straight and your head held steady. This is optimal for focus. Once in this position, you can draw a deep breath through your nose into the belly and fill up your lungs as you would a bottle of water; from the bottom to the top. Exhalation is exactly the opposite: you exhale from your mouth, emptying the lungs from the top to the bottom, and pushing out that last bit of stale air. Repeat this three times.

Once the body is under control and breathing has been harmonized, you can then best control the mind. Now ask the mind, "What would a happy samurai do right now?"

The answer may help you move on from a lust for something that you know to be out of harmony with your best self.

It's that simple... but not easy! Our triggers to lust run deep in our psyche. This technique works better and better the more you practice it. It won't even work all of the time, but it will work some of the time, and you'll become stronger (and happier) as a result.

Gluttony

The "Mac Attack" was a weekly event during our school's rugby season. We had a buddy who worked at the local McDonald's, and he'd give us the Friends and Family deal. While one burger, fries, and a thick banana-flavored shake would suffice, we'd gorge on a double order of everything. We'd look forward to the weekly feast, but we'd all feel utterly miserable shortly after. No amount of negative experience changed the cycle. It was just a collective bad habit, and we all thought it was funny.

Food quite often triggers a comfort response; we sometimes find consolation in eating. Comfort food brings us a sense of comfort, hence the name. As hunter-gatherers, we were designed to eat and keep moving, often gorging on a supply of fruit or berries that were available today but would not necessarily be tomorrow. As a result, we have insulin spikes that used to reward this behavior but can now be as addictive as powerful drugs.

We are designed to survive in a harsh environment, where our body responds to hunger or an attack. Fight or flight. Eat up whenever you can. The problem we face today is we often have an abundance of food available to us and (most of us) do not live in an environment where we are seriously concerned about being attacked every day. If we continue to live in survival mode in today's environment, we will exhaust ourselves, because we won't ever "switch off" the adrenaline needed for fight or flight that was previously reserved for those moments when we actually needed it.

When we are in survival mode and overeating, we create massive amounts of stress on the body. This can become a descending spiral as we get more and more stressed about our weight or health.

Understanding that we don't need to eat more than three meals a day theoretically allows us to manage this, but the habit of binge eating and overeating is difficult to shake. A technique I often use is the same technique we use at the start of each Seido karate class: Gassho.

When you place your palms together, fingers pointing up, there is a physical calmness that follows the motion. This is Gassho. There's a reason why people put their hands together to pray. It is a humbling gesture and dissipates feelings of wanting, which, in turn, generates feelings of gratitude.

As the hands come together in Gassho, close your eyes and take three deep breaths as described previously. Appreciate the abundant world we live in. Appreciate that you have plenty to eat and no longer need to binge-eat in fear of not eating for days or weeks. Feel full and blessed and happy.

Greed

Our old "Mac Attack" sessions didn't involve sharing. When I look back, I think how much more meaningful those meals would have been, if we'd been more mature and able to relish the opportunity to share, plus order significantly less food, as a result.

At the very root of greed is a desire to satiate an appetite. What are we hungry for? Greed is usually associated with money, but greed is also married with an unwillingness to share. Greed is an inward focus rather than an outward focus. Greed asks, "What's in it for me?"

When we train at Seido Karate, we wear a plain white gi (uniform), and the individual wealth of each student is superfluous. We share the floor, and we train together. There is no place for greed on the dojo floor. We carry this spirit into our daily lives, but we don't live our lives within the walls of the dojo. We live in a world where greed drives the very economy we depend on.

The modern economy works on the basis of growth. This economic growth is not for the sake of sustainability, but is growth driven by the greed and desire of shareholders. This economic greed demands and desires constant growth and better returns. Greed requires more than is necessary and more than is required to prosper. Greed can never be fully satiated, so it makes us feel even more desire to satisfy that appetite. Businesses believe, if you're not growing, you're dying.

When we believe we are in a competitive environment of "growth or die," we go into survival mode. While this is a mode that stimulates our basic instincts and often rewards us with feelings of victory or conquest, it creates a cycle of selfishness and celebrates the lowest form of our best self. We exhaust the natural "fight or flight" survival instincts we are born with (to survive in the wilderness) in a charade that will never truly satisfy us or make us happy.

I'm not saying that making money is bad. Quite the opposite. We all need to make money. When the intention to make money is to support a family, help the community, build for the future, or realize something that is driven from the heart, the act of making money is not only noble but absolutely essential. I hope to make money by writing this book, but the intention is to educate and inform… not to get more cash to buy "stuff" with.

When we understand that greed for greed's sake never satisfies or satiates the desire, we can start to identify what it is we are really hungry for. That hunger is our sense of purpose and the realization of our higher self. Our higher self is motivated by the heart rather than by survival. When we choose to thrive rather than survive, we change that paradigm and find ourselves less greedy for "stuff" and more driven to share and think outside of ourselves.

Think of sharing a bottle of wine (or a pitcher of lemonade on a hot day). It always tastes better when you share, and the satisfaction is driven by happiness rather than a feeling of possession. The simple act of sharing subdues greed. My friends and I missed that opportunity in the "Mac Attack" days.

Sloth

I was a lazy student in high school. I'd do my homework on the bus and spend the evenings playing sport or doing karate. I was physically fit, but I limited my mental growth by coasting along and doing the bare minimum to get a decent mark and avoid suspicion from my parents.

This felt like a winning formula until I left school and started my officer training in the Air Force. I was able to handle the physical challenges of basic training, but the study of military law, current international affairs, and military history became a massive challenge, because I had poor study disciplines. I was lucky to have smart, hardworking course mates to help me out.

Many martial artists who train consistently would not consider sloth to be a personal issue to address, but this is false modesty. Sloth is not just physical laziness; it also includes mental laziness. One of Kaicho's many repeated mantras is, "Seven times down, eight times up," and this applies to everything in life. A non-quitting spirit is fostered through the repeated act of not quitting. In a dojo environment, this can be physically tested relatively easily by having students do push-ups to a breaking point and then seeing if the students try to continue or whether they give up.

So, how do we create practical training to develop and test our mental laziness? We should look proactively for challenges to test our resolve and determination. I'm not suggesting picking fights or putting ourselves into dangerous situations; I'm suggesting we look at day-to-day challenges as opportunities to test our happy samurai spirit. It's a challenge. We often joke that when something is difficult or problematic, it's "part of your training," but this is very true. Whenever we approach a challenge with a clear head and the intention to not quit, we are always creating a scenario where we can be proud of ourselves.

Sloth is less about sheer laziness and more about a lack of motivation. When we are not focused on a mission or goal, we can lack motivation, but the very act of training teaches us to just carry on. Move forward. Keep going.

When I wake up, the first thing I do is make the bed. I've been doing this since I was in the military, and it represents a sense of purpose/action from the get-go. It's a small thing to make a bed, but it represents an unwillingness to be lazy and embraces a discipline to be free. It sounds like a contradiction in terms, but discipline (even small disciplines like making the bed) allows us to be free. My RNZAF basic training instructor,

Corporal Smith, used to say, "Gears before beers," and I have always remembered this simple saying.

If I set the alarm on my phone for an early start, I get out of bed when the alarm goes off. This is not a big deal, but hitting the snooze button acknowledges that your decision to set the alarm is no longer a priority. You effectively dishonor your own choices when you decide to disregard your own actions to set the alarm in the first place. The easiest way to develop this habit is to place the phone (or alarm clock) where you would have to get out of bed to reach it, in order to turn off the alarm. Who said all this happy samurai stuff was difficult (or easy)? You might not be happy getting out of bed, but you will be happy you did it, guaranteed!

Wrath

Most of us don't consider ourselves to be wrathful, unless we're particularly self-aware. We might not hold a grudge or have a life-long enemy who is owed a vendetta, but we are still susceptible to wrath.

Just think about the last time somebody cut you off as you drove peacefully down the freeway. Your sense of fierce indignation flares up. You feel angry and upset. You might even select a few choice words as you curse the terrible driver who mindlessly cut you off, demanding instant retribution from the universe. There's a part of you (okay, I'm talking about myself here) that wishes a cop would suddenly appear and drag the offending driver to jail without trial. This is wrath in action.

While the Bible talks about turning the other cheek, this is easier said than done. Kumite (free sparring) trains us to fight with a peaceful mind that accepts that we are exchanging technique with a kohai or fellow student. While avoiding the deliberate injury of our opponent, we still try to strike target areas with controlled technique. If our training partner lands a technique, this is a learning experience for us, not a failure. If we are to spar only with partners whom we know we can overwhelm or beat, there is very little chance for growth and nothing to learn. While it is important to push students from time to time, I believe that kumite should always be practiced at a level that is a very slight degree higher than the level of the junior or least-experienced student. This develops confidence as well as fighting technique and a dojo full of comradery.

When we perceive that someone has done something "against" us, we often react with a wrathful response. In kumite, we develop an acknowledgement when someone lands a strong or well-executed technique. A simple, "Osu," and a bow recognizes the technique and at the same time reminds our ego that the fight does not need to escalate as a result.

The same principle can be applied to the scenario where someone has cut us off on the freeway. While we're not acknowledging good technique, we can get out of our own defensive mode and acknowledge that the person is (most likely) not trying to hurt or harm us. Maybe they are rushing to perform surgery or have a woman in the car about to give birth. We never know what is going on in other people's lives.

Obviously, when someone is trying to hurt or harm you, you need to defend yourself, but we too often perceive this without the threat actually being a reality. Even if someone has hurt you, wrath and vengeance are empty and bitter rewards that bring only a small degree of short-term satisfaction, but never any happiness. Bringing our hands together and appreciating our own happiness allows us to have empathy for others and, as a result, less need for wrath.

By the way—I bring my hands together in "Gassho" a lot, when I'm driving (and not moving).

Envy

At high school, I was always envious of the "rich kids" from the other side of town. These "city-side" kids lived in big houses and drove their own cars. My friends and I didn't have big houses. We borrowed our parents' cars, if we were lucky. This feeling of being "without" made me feel insecure. This feeling of being "without" often made me forget that I lived within walking distance of the beach. I would often forget about all of the wonderful things I had in my life, because I was looking across the harbor bridge at someone else's life. Looking back, not having my own car probably saved my life, but envy could often steal some of the joy from my life.

The twenty-first-century world we live in constantly trains us to be envious. We read and watch messages that tell us we "deserve" this or "need" that. We're told to "stay ahead" and not to get "behind" in our school life and in our work life. Just who are we trying to get ahead of? When we compare ourselves with someone else, our ego takes over, and we forget ourselves. This preoccupation with comparing ourselves to others leads us to a false sense of self-importance. This is the way of the narcissist and egomaniac. It brings no joy.

Competition is fun and a healthy part of development, but it can lead us down a spiral into a feeling that we need to live in survival mode. We feel we need to beat out the competition or we'll miss out. This is the antithesis of happiness.

To be grateful for what we have is to be rich. To be ungrateful for what we have is to be poor. What is in your bank account has nothing to do with the universal truth of these two simple sentences.

Let's look at Tom Brady, former New England Patriots quarterback (now with the 2021-winning Tampa Bay Buccaneers), owner of multiple Super Bowl rings, and husband to supermodel Gisele Bündchen. It's easy to be envious of Tom.

It's not a case of looking at Tom's life and dissecting what we have that Tom doesn't have. We don't need to discount what Tom has and belittle what he's achieved to make ourselves feel better. It shouldn't bring us any pleasure to know that some fans might yell at Tom and some players on opposing teams might even try to hurt Tom. Tom plays a dangerous game and risks getting badly hurt in practice and on the playing field. This is Tom's life.

We are not living Tom's life and nor should we be. We all have a duty to do justice to our own lives and allow others to live theirs. We are always best served being ourselves... because everyone else is taken. Envy raises its ugly head when we're unsure about ourselves and compare ourselves to others because we lack clarity of our purpose and identity. The ego takes over our sense of inner peace. We feel ungrateful for our "lot in life" as we compare and consider what we don't have.

Think about someone special in your life, whether they are alive or no longer with us. Think of your relationship with that person and recognize that you and you alone know the depth and beauty of that relationship. That's yours. Your gratitude for this makes you rich. Your gratitude for this will make you happier, and your gratitude for this will amplify similar feelings of gratitude for other things in your life that exist now and will exist in the future.

If you're reading this book, you've been educated beyond ninety-five percent of all humans who have ever lived, so you're blessed. If you took a shower this morning and used a bathroom, you're one of the same small group of lucky humans who live with that privilege each and every day. Again, we're not comparing ourselves to those wonderful humans who lived (and still live) without basic education and sanitation, but we're grateful for what we have and recognize this as special rather than "deserved" or something to be taken for granted.

An easy exercise to feel and manifest gratitude every single day is to close your eyes in the shower and simply be grateful for the hot water. This takes less than five seconds. Gratitude is the arch nemesis of envy. You can't be mad or full of envy when you feel grateful. Gassho to the rescue.

Pride

Whenever I met the rich kids from the city at school balls and sports events, I'd desperately try to impress them. I was very insecure about my life when compared to theirs. I had no idea they were going through exactly the same growing pains and problems. I had no idea that many of those big houses they lived in had big problems as well. My ability to have any sort of empathy was stymied by pride. Some of those "rich kids" are still my closest friends today. I have learned so much from them about the foolish limits of my own assumptions.

Pride, when it involves comparing and recognizing the development in your new self with that of your old (or older) self, is a good thing. Pride, when we start to posture or strut, is the very essence of insecurity. Think about the last time you met or engaged with someone who was trying to pump themselves up by telling you how great they were. Were you impressed? Quite the opposite. The irony is, the harder we try to pump ourselves up to be impressive to others, the more insecure and insincere we appear. A tiger doesn't need to tell anyone they are a tiger.

Kaicho reminds us to remember "Shoshin" (beginner's mind), when we approach our training. In a dojo environment, there is a tendency to want to be seen as one of the best or strongest fighters or technicians.

This is pure ego. The practice of "Shoshin" teaches us to start and finish every action or activity with a calm mind. The battle with pride is internal not external.

When observing someone who trains hard and conscientiously, we feel and experience the sincerity of that person, and we trust and follow that example. The opposite is true when we observe someone who is trying to be impressive or trying to convince others of their strength or prowess. Our goal is to manage our own ego, so the pride we have in ourselves is personal and within us, rather than something we need to express to the outside world.

The weakness of our pride is often revealed during competition. Our character and ego are revealed in how we humbly acknowledge defeat rather than how we celebrate victory. It is easy to celebrate and be magnanimous when we win. It is harder to be humble and gracious in defeat. This is what a warrior spirit is all about. My niece, Laura Mariu, was captain of the New Zealand rugby league team in 2017, when they lost the World Cup final to Australia. Of the many achievements this marvelous woman has experienced, her speech at the end of the match, when she congratulated Australia and acknowledged her teammates, is one of the most impressive to me. Pride in oneself, with empathy and humility, is both powerful and beautiful.

When taking promotion from brown belt to black belt, Kaicho has students wear a white belt from the time they are asked to take promotion until the final day of the test. This is also done for each successive dan (black belt) grade promotion. We all understand the theory of "Shoshin," but can we physically embrace this by training in the dojo with a white belt on as a "novice" or "beginner"? Every day and every class present a lesson to us. Are we receptive to that lesson with a beginner's mind? If so, we have so much to learn. If not, there is little to learn. In the beginner's mind, the opportunities are endless. In the "expert's" mind, the possibilities are limited.

The test of our command over pride is our ability to be our best self without the need for reward or recognition. Service to others for no reward achieves this. Helping a stranger. Donating anonymously. We will ultimately be happier knowing who we are and being proud of that person rather than trying to impress other people with our self-promoting story. A happy samurai doesn't need to tell anyone they are a happy samurai.

So, what happened after I taxied my Strikemaster into the 14 Squadron bay that evening? I filled in the flight report sheet at the ground crew desk, and I reported the over-speed of the air-brakes. I was one of two teenagers on the squadron at the time, so I got a few sideways looks from some of the more senior ground crew staff. The ground crew were up late for night flying and in no mood for young rookies like me busting their jets. These people dedicated their lives to keeping these older jets flying safely. I felt guilty, but I was glad I'd reported the over-speed.

I had a meeting with the Wing Commander the next day. My course mates gave me moral support as I got ready to face the music. I thought about the inevitable check flight or even being chopped from my wings course.

The Wing Commander got straight to the point and informed me that an air-break over-speed was not a critical stress but a stress nonetheless. He asked me why I reported the over-speed. I simply said it was the right thing to do and what we've been told to do. He didn't smile but simply said, "Don't do it again," and told me to get back to work.

I never over-sped the air-brakes again. I had learned a valuable lesson through that experience. Stay present, and do the right thing. I never divulged my ruminations about using my Martin-Baker ejection seat that night, either. Until now.

1: Courage

"Courage, above all things, is the first quality of a warrior."

—Sun Tzu

To be a warrior, one needs courage.

On September 11, 2001, Captain Pat "Paddy" Brown (FDNY) and eleven men from Ladder 3 responded to the attacks on the World Trade Center. The 3-Truck's firehouse is located near the Twin Towers site, so these men were some of the very first responders on the scene.

The 9/11 disaster, in which so many people tragically perished, was also one of the most heroic and courageous rescue missions in U.S. history. Over 25,000 people were safely evacuated from the World Trade Center on that terrible day. The bravery and courage of the first responders saved thousands of lives and gave comfort to many more in those last moments before they were lost.

Captain Pat is one of my heroes and someone who represents the epitome of courage. At the age of seventeen, Pat persuaded his father to allow him to sign up for the U.S. Marines, and he went off to Vietnam on a combat assignment. He became a highly decorated Marine Sergeant before returning to civilian life. In 1977, Pat joined the FDNY (Ladder 26) and later joined Manhattan's elite Rescue Company One. He then travelled to Brooklyn and joined Rescue Two. Sensei Pat was also a student at Seido Karate and was a kind and generous kohai and an instructor in the blind program.

It is believed that Pat and his men were on the fortieth floor of the North Tower when it fell. As his team continued to face their fears while ascending to rescue more people, Pat's last recorded words were, "Thank you."

I don't use the word "warrior" lightly. I have enormous respect for the true warriors who face life and death on a daily basis. These people, like Pat, are our example. First responders, in particular, are such courageous and heroic people. We should all try to emulate that warrior spirit when it comes to embracing courage.

I have served in the RNZAF (Royal New Zealand Air Force) as a pilot, as well as in the RNZA (Royal New Zealand Army) Territorial Force as an air dispatch officer, but I have never faced life-or-death situations on a daily basis for an extended period of time. I am awed by service personnel who deal with trauma as part of their day-to-day jobs. We should collectively support and honor these courageous souls.

So, what does courage mean to a happy samurai living in the twenty-first century?

Courage is our ability to do something that frightens us. Courage is about having strength in the face of pain or grief. Courage is about being vulnerable. One can only be vulnerable with courage.

One of the five dojo kun mentioned in the introduction is, "To guard against impetuous courage." We should not jump into things carelessly and without thought. Everything starts and finishes with stillness. Even when that stillness is for a split second, we can act with courage immediately thereafter, but without an impetuous lack of thought or care. Otherwise, we might end up ejecting out of a fully serviceable aircraft.

Courage requires a decision to face fear and address it head on. Courage does not allow us to shy away from the challenges we face each and every day. If something is dangerous and life-threatening, we should run. To stand in front of a tornado is not courageous—it is foolish. Courage in the context of a happy samurai is our willingness and enthusiasm to look at a situation, pause, and then address it directly and with our best effort, because we refuse to ignore the challenge that is presented to us.

During promotions (from white belt through all dan grades), Kaicho asks each student to stand up and speak in front of the group, which includes other candidates and any senior students "witnessing" and supporting them. Kaicho asks each student to talk from their heart. He is not interested in discovering who has the best oratory skills or who can tell the funniest stories; he wants to see the courage of each person to be vulnerable and to speak from their very heart.

I have always found this vulnerability to be the most challenging and difficult part of every promotion. I recall hard physical and mental challenges throughout my various karate tests, but the vulnerability to stand up and talk from my heart has always taken more courage than facing down a strong fighter in kumite or performing a kata with my eyes closed in the early hours of the morning.

To develop courage in our daily lives, we are challenged to become more vulnerable. Throughout our lives, we have all developed incredible tools for self-preservation, and some of these are essential for life in the modern age. If neither you nor I knew how to survive, we wouldn't be communicating right now. The question for the happy samurai is can we evolve our mindset from one that survives to one that thrives?

Many of the self-preservation tactics we have developed over the course of our lives can limit our ability to move forward from those specific situations and feelings that were needed in order to deal with something in the past, but we no longer need to deal with today.

I remember the first time I stood up in front of an audience and performed. (I was just a kid at a Christmas party.) I felt nervous and shy and uncomfortable. All justifiable feelings. I forgot the words of the song. I lacked the courage to be vulnerable then, but I can embrace it more easily now. I am no longer a small child. I know the consequences aren't dire, if I forget my lines or stutter a little or forget something or make a mistake. That's fine. If we look forward rather than back, we remove those feelings of nervous survival and replace them with a positive willingness to thrive..., mistakes included.

When facing a challenge at work, at home, in sport, or with any other activity in life within our community, embrace it! Be grateful for that opportunity to give something your best shot, regardless of the result. You might achieve something you didn't think was possible. Or you might not achieve your desired "goal" but learn a lot in the process. It's a win-win scenario. You achieve or learn. Courage will bring you to a place of personal growth, so eat it up whenever you get the chance. Those closest to you will appreciate your authentic self so much more than a protected wall of "safety" barriers. I know this from personal experience.

I experienced a lot of grief in my early twenties. My father died when I was twenty-two, and in the space of three years, three close friends and fellow Air Force pilots died. I was determined not to feel that pain again, so I created a wall of invulnerability to protect myself. I still maintained a sense of humor but drank a lot and masked much of my grief with jovial partying. One of my favorite expressions at the time was, "Party on," and I said this a lot. I am blessed to still have many friends now whom I had all those years ago. Much of this continued friendship is about their patience rather than mine, so I am very grateful for this. I was closed off and unavailable for anything near to vulnerability.

A degree of mourning is absolutely necessary when someone close to us dies. We miss them. We still love them. We must also find a time to celebrate their life and be grateful for the time we had with them. Our ego will justify being closed off and invulnerable, because it makes us feel like we are in control of the situation. The truth could not be more opposite. We are not in control of when people leave us or when we will die, but we are in control of how we choose to address loss with courage. It took me more than twenty years to figure this out, so I am desperately hopeful that you can apply this knowledge to your life and avoid the longer-term processing I went through.

While closed off from any real intimate connection, I convinced myself I was strong and determined. I thought I was fearless in the face of life's tragedies, because I wouldn't allow my heart to be hurt by any of them. I thought I was courageous, but I was not living. I was metaphorically treading water and missing the joy of swimming. Life is for living not for avoiding. We cannot experience love if we cannot express love from within our heart. When we try to protect ourselves through fear, we move away from our authentic self and become a shell of who we are meant to be: our true self.

Courage and vulnerability are not necessarily about winning or losing a battle or a fight. If we have the courage to show up and do our very best without having any direct control over the outcome, we are being truly courageous. Think of the last time you did something courageous. You took a risk, you faced fear, and you didn't know or control the result. The more we practice this type of vulnerability, the more courage we will naturally apply to our life, as a habit. We develop more confidence to face our fears, because we know we can do it and we don't need to doubt ourselves or our ability to face fear.

I remember training with the late (Shuseki Shihan) William Oliver in the late 1990s. I would travel to his uptown dojo on Manhattan's Broadway with my training partner, Hakim Walker. I would look forward to the tough fighting environment in the dojo, but there was always a degree of trepidation before kumite. There were many seasoned fighters in the dojo who were bigger, stronger, and more experienced than I was. I was humbled and a little intimidated. This is a natural and healthy feeling when developing fighting skills, as we all need to be pushed to get better over time. The courage to face this fear is what Shuseki instilled in all of his students. This very physical aspect of courage also develops our mental ability to face our fears and go beyond them. The fear often remains but gets less and less over time.

Rejection is also a big fear in this modern world. Whether you're making sales calls or casting for a role in a movie, the fear of rejection is very real and hinders our growth potential. Not surprisingly, in the world of movies, actors who are the most vulnerable are most venerated. Salespeople with the most authentic love for their product sell more product than those who "fake it until they make it," with hearts that are just not in it. Courage helps us to overcome this fear of rejection and step forward to give it our best effort, regardless of our ability to control the result.

To do what we love, we need to love what we do. This doesn't represent an idealistic "perfect" job or activity that never presents challenges or obstacles. Quite the opposite. When we have the courage to accept challenges and obstacles in the pursuit of our mission or goal, we can truly love what we do. Love will always conquer fear. Fear is an obstacle to finding love in what we do, so the courage to remove this fear will allow us to become more vulnerable and be more "in love" with what we do.

When we look back on life's tough lessons, we can become depressed, if this is too much of our focus. When we look forward toward some of the "worst-case scenarios" we dream up in our head, we can become anxious, if this is too much of our focus. Fear of repeating the past or fear of the unknown future can stop us from being courageous. If we are in the present, these fears and anxieties have less sway, which enables us to act with courage as we face (whether real or imagined) what confronts us. When we are present, our focus is on the here and now (the only time we can actually do anything), so our ability to respond is the best opportunity we ever have to "control" the situation through our actions (or inaction).

Sparring requires us to be very present. If we dwell on an earlier sparring session or a technique that's just been landed, we are drawn away from the present moment and cannot be as sure of our actions in both offense and defense. When we allow our minds to drift to the next fight or to a technique we want to execute, (regardless of the opportunity to actually do so), we lose focus on the job at hand. Being present becomes easier with practice but is always a challenge, as our ego constantly reminds us that we are set in our ways and the future will continue to be the same as the past. This is not true. Our future is available to us as a happy samurai, if we can conquer fear through courage.

To step forward into the unknown takes a great deal of courage. We know what we have experienced, but we have no idea about our absolute potential in the future. We are all insecure in some way, and we all lack self-confidence in certain situations. This is what makes us human. I think about all those "rich kids" of whom I was so envious and who remain some of my dearest friends. Today's task is to work toward being a better person, a happier samurai, and a more productive member of our community. Karate-Do is a "way" rather than a destination or end goal. Don't beat yourself up—just keep moving forward.

The fact that you are reading this book is a testament to your wanting to develop yourself and shows you do not believe you have all the answers. None of us have all the answers! We are all students of life until the day we die. It takes courage to address the fact that we don't actually have all the answers. In order to evolve and develop as humans, there are things we have to learn and things we need to let go of, in order to grow. To realize our true potential, we must leave our old self. This old self is a very secure and known quantity that our ego will fiercely protect. Sometimes we need to choose between security and freedom.

Our best self is free and happy. If you can honestly say that you are completely free and happy, then I salute you and encourage you to keep working to maintain that. For the rest of us, our best self awaits, if we have the courage to face our ego and step forward into the unknown. Even when our history is full of negative things that we now have the ability to change, we often don't do it, because we are scared of what the alternative is. We are not too lazy to change; we have a fear of change. Our lack of confidence enables this fear to keep us captive in our past history, rather than allow us to move toward our best potential and a more positive future.

One of Kaicho's meditation lectures is, "Onore o hige sezu." This translates as, "Don't underestimate yourself." This is not an invitation to put yourself up on a pedestal and think you can simply do anything you please. This is an invitation to gain confidence in your ability to face your fears and step forward to address those fears by your thoughts and actions.

We all laugh at the "You can do it!" meme, but this resonates with all of us. We can do it. We know we can do it, but we all need to challenge ourselves to make facing fear a priority. When we do, we can raise the bar on what we can achieve, regardless of the fears that currently hold us back. Do not shy away. You are capable of more than you think. Bend under the pressure then jump up and be your best self.

There is a difference between humility and constant self-deprecation. While humility manages our ego and acknowledges that we should adopt a modest view of our own sense of self-importance, self-deprecation is an ego-driven criticism of our best self. When we hear ourselves saying, "I'm not 'smart' enough," or "I'm not 'good' enough," this is not humility, but a negative reinforcement based on fear. Whenever fear motivates our thoughts or actions, we need to be courageous to overcome it. Fear never delivers our true potential, but only a weaker, lesser version of us.

Back yourself. The best investment you can ever make is an investment in yourself. This might sound very selfish, but the courage to take care of others is directly proportional to your ability to face your own fears through personal growth. You are capable of wonderful things that you might not even be able to imagine right now. This is a fact. All we need to do to become more courageous is to progressively face our fears and overcome them one by one. As we develop our own courage, we can better serve our family, our workplace, and the community that surrounds us.

Like the instruction we receive at the start of a commercial flight, we all need to attend to our own oxygen before we can be in a position to help others. Without an ability to face our fears, it is impossible for us to help others do the same. To be a role model and a constructive member of our society, we all need to represent the best of ourselves through the courage to be vulnerable, authentic, and genuine.

To be true to ourselves takes courage. If we stand up to sexism or racism or if someone is talking badly about a friend who isn't present to defend themselves, we are doing something courageous. Sometimes this courage might incur the displeasure or even ridicule of others, but the alternative is to live in conflict with our true selves and to dishonor who we are. Courage is relatively easy, if we don't fear the thoughts of others. When we no longer fear what people might think of us if we are true to ourselves, we become more courageous. Courage is much easier to embrace when we have our ego in check, but this is a constant struggle, and we all know how hard this battle can be.

To develop courage, begin with relatively small things that you fear. You might not want to make a brief speech at a friend's birthday party. You might not want to admit to a person you are close to that you were wrong, because you think it will make you look weak. You might not want to do a yoga class, because you fear looking foolish due to your lack of experience. These are fears that are all valid. Do all of these things anyway! Just face it and walk through it. I have a fear that I won't sell a single copy of this book. I'm still writing. Just keep going.

When it comes to fear and courage, it is easy for us to recognize this in other people. We are objective about others but seldom have the same degree of self-awareness to be equally objective about our own fears. We often observe lessons that would apply to other people, particularly to those close to us. These are the lessons we need to be paying attention to. These lessons are for us. Remember: the lessons we teach best are the lessons we need to learn most. Have the courage to be self-aware. Develop the courage to recognize that those life lessons that resonate with us are directly addressing us.

Setting goals takes courage. When setting your own goals, a traditional Japanese daruma doll is a wonderful talisman. A daruma doll is modeled after Bodhidharma

(Daruma in Japan), the founder of the Zen tradition of Buddhism.

The daruma doll comes with no eyes. You set your goal and draw (or paint) one eye on the daruma doll. Every time you look at the daruma doll, you are reminded that you have work to do and your goal is still in front of you, if you persevere.

When you achieve your goal, you draw the second eye on the doll's face to remind yourself that you can do what you set your mind to and that you should be confident to set more goals and keep moving forward. A daruma doll also wobbles when disturbed, but it always sets itself straight. A daruma doll is a beautiful gift for friends and family as a symbol of good luck.

When it comes to courage, look at vulnerability as strength rather than weakness, because vulnerability is our greatest measure of courage. Captain Pat Brown understood that and applied that courage throughout his heroic life.

1: Benevolence

(or Compassion)

"Service to others is the rent you pay for your room here on Earth."

—Muhammad Ali

I hadn't slept for three days. I hadn't eaten much, either. I struggled in the dark as fifty-knot winds blew sheets of water through my flimsy tent. My one-man tent was pitched on the side of a small hill in the desert outside of Waiouru. I had to fix the tent to protect myself from the elements, or I would expose myself to hypothermia. I was a trained soldier and fit. I was also exhausted and exasperated by the swirling madness around me. I needed help. *Why on Earth did I join the Army anyway?*

After I left the Air Force, I was offered a position as a Territorial Force (TF) officer at the Army's 5 Movement Squadron. Having completed my officer training in the Air Force, I was offered the position as a Second Lieutenant. The role involved working with air dispatch at an Air Force base that I was already familiar with. Our task was to load and dispatch (usually out of a C-130 Hercules) specialized equipment for the SAS. It was exciting work. I was to work with full-time professional soldiers, so I opted to go through Army officer training and brush up on my appreciation for all things Army.

During my sleep-deprivation exercise, deep into my Army officer training, I found myself in gale-force winds on the side of a hill. I struggled to resurrect my tent. I couldn't see more than ten feet in front of me in the howling wind.

A dark shadow approached me that materialized into Staff Sergeant Var Tui Tui, who was running the exercise. "Are you missing those steaks at the mess, Air Force?"

All I could muster was, "Yes, Staff." Then he proceeded to help me get the tent back into some sort of shape before shoveling me into it. As he shuffled back into the storm, I yelled, "Thanks, Staff!" and fell asleep. The first sleep I'd had in three days.

Staff Sergeant Var Tui Tui was a decorated veteran who had served in Vietnam and Borneo. He was a hardened, professional soldier who had been in the New Zealand Army's infantry corps for more than twenty-five years. He often gave me a hard time, but I sensed an appreciation for the fact that I had volunteered to do the Army officer training course. One of the strange things about sleep deprivation is it can make everything seem very funny. I wouldn't appreciate Staff Var Tui Tui's compassion and benevolence until the sun came up the next day, and we realized we'd been in the middle of a tornado.

The Dalai Lama once said, "If you want others to be happy, practice compassion. If you want to be happy, practice compassion."

When warriors train hard, becoming fast and strong, they are no longer "normal" people. They develop a power that must be used for good and for service to others. When an opportunity to help others is not immediately at hand, the happy samurai will go out of their way to find one. As the Dalai Lama puts it, "Compassion is the wish to see others free from suffering."

Much like the tenet of righteousness, benevolence carries a responsibility to provide service to others and often requires a degree of self-sacrifice, as well. This is not to say that a happy samurai forgets his own path and gives it up for others. Quite the opposite. The happy samurai's path is to help others. The work is benevolent as well as rewarding, because it carries with it the feeling of purpose and the sense of fulfillment in the mission.

It feels good to earn your happiness. Service to others, as Muhammad Ali put it, earns your rent for your place on Earth. You've earned your spot. I have this Ali quote stuck to the back of my front door, because I can be forgetful and need this as a daily reminder. When you give service to others, you should be proud of that and proud of yourself for making the world a better place as a result of your being in it. The world needs more people like you. Imagine a world full of happy samurai—what a wonderful, strong, dynamic, powerful, and invigorating world that would be. You can create that world for yourself through benevolence.

Another meditation lecture of Kaicho's that had a big impact on me is, "Ataeru ukeru shiyawase," which translates to, "Giving is necessary for happiness." When we give something to somebody from our heart, without expecting anything in return, we are walking the path of benevolence. The reward we receive from developing a benevolent spirit is not exterior but is within us. We feel a sense of happiness when we do good things. We earn a sense of peace and harmony that unconditional giving brings. We are contributing to a better world.

We often feel the need for something or we want more of something. This can be for love, financial security, trust, respect, attention, or any number of things we believe we lack or would benefit from, if we had more. A benevolent spirit recognizes, if we want more love, we only have to give more love. If we want more trust, we have to give more trust. If we want more attention, we have to give more attention. This is the nature of giving.

When we give to others with an open heart, it is difficult (if not impossible) to be selfish and feel less fortunate. Why should we feel less fortunate if we have the ability to give? Giving makes our spirit rich. When we give, we are exponentially more likely to receive something similar to what we are giving. Try it... It works!

We've all heard that expression, "What goes around comes around." It resonates with us because we know it to be true. It's not a case of deserve or not deserve; it's a simple case of energy and attitude. Hard work is rewarded with a sense of accomplishment and a pride in one's own ability to work hard and endure obstacles and challenges. Whatever is worth having and anything that is revered comes from hard work. When something is quickly attained and easily achieved, it does not carry the same value as that which has been earned. When we give, we are working harder and more diligently than when we are receiving.

How much "stuff" do we need to be happy? We are all guilty of wanting material objects. I know I am. When we get caught up in today's consumerist cycle, we find that our appetite is never fully satiated; we always feel that we need more. The short-term high from something "new" quickly evaporates as that thing becomes "old," even before we're aware of it. This is a sense of being "without" and is not a happy state of being. When we appreciate what we have and find ourselves in a position to give, we are in a state of kindness and happiness.

The famous Mister Rogers once said, "There are three ways to ultimate success: The first way is to be kind. The second way is to be kind. The third way is to be kind." When we are kindhearted, our mind, body, and spirit are in harmony and at peace. This is the very essence of bushido training. At Seido Karate, we train our mind and our body to be strong so both can support and strengthen a spirit that is generous and kind. A magnanimous spirit is developed and strengthened over time; it is the polar opposite of the spirit of an insecure bully.

A magnanimous spirit is both generous and forgiving, especially toward a rival or someone less powerful. It becomes clearly obvious to those around us when we are insecure and lacking in kindness. Conversely, when we are kind, we bring positive energy toward us, and we gain the respect and appreciation of others through our actions, rather than through simply what we say. When we are in contact with people who are weaker or less powerful (whatever the circumstance), we command more respect and appreciation by treating them kindly rather than lording over them, being insecure bullies. We cannot hide our intentions behind false words, so the magnanimous spirit must be fostered within, so it can find its own expression through our actions.

As the world appears to go faster and faster, we can feel more and more separated. This feeling of isolation is most common in big cities, where people adopt a survival mode through a fear of scarce resources and a lack of abundance. The simple act of giving brings us into contact with people. We cannot be alone when we are giving someone attention, being kind, or helping someone. It's impossible! So, whenever you're feeling lonely, simply think of who you can express your kindness to, and you'll cease being lonely. Like all of these principles, the more you do it, the more easily it manifests into your daily life.

Benevolence is a core part of the training curriculum at Seido Karate. Kaicho leads community-driven projects through walking meditation, where students join him as he presents food and gifts to the local homeless shelters in New York. We can all feel sorry for ourselves from time to time, but these experiences teach us to be grateful for what we have and bring to light the reality that we are blessed to live the lives we have. The more we embrace this reality, the more likely we are to give. The more likely we are to be kind. The more likely we are to be happy.

The Seido Juku Benefit Foundation is a nonprofit organization run by Kaicho and his son, Nidaime. Founded in 1987, this foundation provides financial support and karate instruction for students who would otherwise be unable to train in karate. This includes the visually impaired, hearing impaired, homeless children, and adults with special needs.

I have had the opportunity to train with these students and instruct classes. Teaching visually impaired students brings with it an appreciation for clear verbal communication and an empathy for how we learn. Teaching hearing-impaired students brings an appreciation for visual communication and demands excellence in stances and technique. I have learned so much from these experiences, so it's not a case of benevolence, but a case of interdependence. We need to give. We need to be connected.

I have taught karate at New York City's YAI (Young Adult Institute) for many years. YAI was launched in 1957 to provide innovative services to New York's I/DD (intellectual and/or developmental disabilities) community. When I started teaching at YAI, my ego was full of self-congratulation. I felt good about doing something benevolent, but the spirit was more self-absorbed than truly magnanimous. Over a very short period of time (about three weeks), I was so humbled by the experience that my attitude changed dramatically. I realized that teaching at the YAI was becoming my happiest time of the week. It was no longer about how wonderful I was for doing this service for the community—it was about how wonderful this opportunity was for teaching me. It was about how much these beautiful people at YAI were teaching me about myself. Even now, the tears well up in my eyes as I appreciate these students and the other instructors within this very special program.

What strikes me most about YAI karate students, in general, is their incredible enthusiasm to learn. When students approach karate with a completely open mind to learning, it is a pure joy to teach them. This is their gift to me. Many of the YAI students I have taught over the years are the antithesis of selfishness. They give constantly with open hearts that are full of love and joy. There is no agenda or motivation other than trying hard to learn and not quitting. What an example of benevolence. I aspire to approach my own training in the same manner, but many YAI students have a far superior grasp on this concept than I have. They are my teachers.

In 2008, Kyoshi Boris Kupermann and Kyoshi Dan Tierney, both United States military veterans, started the Seido Veterans program to provide martial arts training for returning service men and women. Their idea in founding the program stemmed from a belief that the spiritual and physical benefits they both receive from their training at Seido would also help this new generation of veterans to integrate themselves back into civilian society. With veterans returning from wars in

Iraq and Afghanistan, this was (and still is) a very important program. The motto of the Seido Veterans Group is: We Are One.

When we give, we are no longer alone.

When we practice benevolence for the sake of doing good rather than to become happy (or rewarded) as a result, something wonderful happens. We experience growth. The very experience of giving creates good energy, and happiness comes as a natural and inevitable byproduct. When we kick our ego to the curb and just give for the sake of giving, we find that the "work" becomes effortless and enjoyable, because it is no longer "work" but something we just do. The positive energy this provides reinforces the motivation to keep doing this, and so it continues to regenerate more energy.

So, when should we start to develop a kinder and more generous spirit so we can feel more connected with the world we live in? Now! Not tomorrow, but today. What is the best use of our time if not to create more positive energy and feel more fulfilled and happier as a result?

We are all guilty of putting things off and procrastinating. We say, "I'll start next month," or, "Next year for sure." We've all said these things to ourselves to justify inaction. Who do you know who could do with some kindness? Try calling someone you think needs some kindness. You'll be amazed at the results.

If you did just call someone, I trust that experience was positive, and it will be a little bit easier to make the same call again.

Whenever we put kind thoughts into physical action, we create something special for somebody else and increase our own capacity to do so. We are not wasting our time. We don't have to be Mother Teresa to make an impact on the world we live in, but her example is one we should acknowledge and be humbled by. Mother Teresa once said, "Give until it hurts." I think this is a beautiful goal for all of us, but it expresses a deeper willingness to go beyond what is "convenient" and really embrace developing a kind and giving spirit by the practice of being proactively generous.

We all pat ourselves on the back from time to time, when we feel we have been generous, and that's not a bad thing. The trick is to keep going. Don't stop and be satisfied that the job is over, because it never is over. It's a journey and a process rather than a set quantity. When we create this natural inclination toward generosity, the world opens up new possibilities to us, and our view of the world becomes more positive and more encouraging. When we continue to give beyond what we thought was required (and beyond what we imagined we were capable of), we step into a future that is more abundant than our past. We create a new reality for ourselves which is more generous and kinder.

A benevolent spirit is the highest form of our natural self, because we are out of "survival mode" and in harmony with our best instincts. We move beyond a purely animal survival instinct and create a more positive, human view of the world. Even dogs understand this. Think about the natural tendency of a dog. They are always happy to see you, excited to play, and willing to please. Dogs have a benevolent spirit. Dogs can be trained to fight, but their natural tendency is to be kind and fun-loving. Dogs can teach us a great deal about unconditional love and a willingness to give.

Our martial arts training should develop a strong fighting spirit, but one that is channeled in the right direction. Kaicho's lecture, "Ushi nomu mizu nu. Hebi nomu mizu doku," translates to, "A cow drinks water and produces milk. A snake drinks water and produces poison." We can misuse our training, if we don't apply it to personal growth. Many students will train hard for a period of time but then quit, because they do not experience the deeper aspects of training. Physical training is important, but without developing the mind and spirit, it has limited application for a more balanced and fulfilling life. Training should develop a character with empathy and compassion. Training should not develop a character that intimidates or scares others.

Part of martial arts training is the cycle of learning and teaching and learning from teaching. A strong karateka will evolve from student to teacher. That karateka recognizes that they will always be a student but also embraces the responsibility to teach. A dojo is developed through the generosity of the seniors. Anyone who has studied martial arts can remember the seniors who made an impact on them when they were beginners. These are the people we need to emulate as we continue with our study and give back to the dojo, in order to pass on the training to the next generation of students.

There is often talk about "old school" training and the understanding that training today is different from yesteryear. Of course, it is. This isn't a good or bad thing; it's simply a fact of life. The fact that martial arts training evolves and changes over time does not negate the essentials of facing physical, mental, and spiritual challenges. Some students are more physically capable than others, but all students have something special that nobody else has. An instructor's job is to recognize the talents and challenges of each student and then push those students to their best potential. An instructor's job is to follow the example of their seniors in terms of the generosity with which they were taught.

Outside the dojo, this generosity can be reflected in how we help or assist people in our day-to-day lives. Think of somebody (outside of a dojo environment) who has had a positive impact on you, and think about who you could "pay that forward" to. When it comes to benevolence, this is the best application of martial arts training. While everyone we come across has something to teach us, we also have the opportunity to be kind and generous to everyone we come into contact with. We don't need to feel the pressure to live like a saint, but we accept the responsibility to just give it our best effort. Don't quit. Be kind. Keep going.

What comes first, motivation or action? We often wait for inspiration before we are motivated into action. Action, on the other hand, motivates us toward something, so it is the action (or inaction) that starts the process, like a spark starts a fire. When we create a habit of initiating kindness, we create a motivating force that will continue to sustain and nurture that instinct to be generous. Not surprisingly, the more we do this, the easier it becomes, as it creates a new habit that we enjoy and that others will appreciate.

It is important to acknowledge those people who contribute toward making our lives better. This gratitude starts with our parents, which will be covered in more detail in the chapter about honor. When we say, "thank you," and show appreciation to those who are kind and generous toward us, we give them a gift. Simultaneously, we are reinforcing our acknowledgement that they are an example for us to follow, to pay forward to others who need our kindness and generosity. The cycle is maintained and reinforced when we "add" back into the positive affirmation of kindness. While we shouldn't always expect to be thanked for our kindness, it certainly feels good when appreciation is given; this perpetuates the desire and motivation to be kind. Saying, "Thank you," is the first step to building a benevolent heart.

Thankfulness, when it becomes a habit, develops more gratitude. Gratitude, which manifests a kind and benevolent heart, is the completion of thankfulness. Thankfulness can be words or an acknowledgement said or written. Gratitude, on the other hand, is expressed by action. This is why it is so important to teach children to say, "Thank you," to develop thankfulness as a habit, so they can experience and express more gratitude.

At the end of each karate class, we bow to each other to show respect. I often remind the children's class that this is for all of us to thank one another. Without a teacher, you can't be a student. Without students, you can't be a teacher. Whether I am teaching karate or taking a class as a student, I thank everyone at the end of class. This is thankfulness. Turning up to the next class and giving my best effort is gratitude.

Having the insight to recognize gratitude, as well as somebody else's point of view, takes compassion. Appreciating someone else's unique life (outside of their role toward us) takes compassion and empathy. Both compassion and empathy can be particularly difficult for younger children, because they often live in a very egocentric world. Mum's job is to be a mum. Dad's job is to be a dad. My karate instructor's job is to be a karate instructor. These people don't have any other role(s) in their life other than the specific role they play in relationship to the child. Does this sound familiar? It is not only children who are guilty of this lack of empath. It is all of us. It is a lesson we all must learn.

I also instruct children in my karate classes to be thankful to their parents. It is a parent's job to provide food and shelter for their children. It is a responsibility. Should this be something that is taken for granted? I do not think so. I ask all of the kids in my class to thank their parents after each meal and to take time to show appreciation to their parents. I even ask them to offer to do the dishes, but I know I'm probably pushing my luck at that stage. The important thing is to look beyond our own sense of self-importance and acknowledge others with a compassionate heart.

It is easy to blame the government, blame the company, or blame the boss. When we play the "blame game," we're looking for an excuse or an out, and we're adopting a victim mentality. This is not the bushido way. We may not agree with the government or with the boss, but we can have some empathy for them and get over some of our beef with them. We have the ability to vote (in America), and we also have the ability to leave our job and find another job or work for ourselves. We have the ability to take action and take responsibility. This is the freedom we gain from benevolence, as we move away from being a victim and embrace empathy and compassion in its place.

As we strive to become more and more humble as well as less ego-driven, compassion replaces anxiety, and empathy replaces arrogance.

My appreciation for Staff Sergeant Var Tui Tui's compassion was finally realized as the sun rose on the Waiouru desert. A herd of wild horses drifted in the distance.

I packed up my tent and surveilled the damage to the surrounding area. Trees had been ripped out of the ground. Bemused Officer Cadets searched the area for scattered equipment. Staff Var Tui Tui had also slept in a tent that night and was the only person in the platoon who looked remotely together.

Staff Var Tui Tui ambled over to me and said, "You okay?" I nodded my head. He then said, "I heard you laughing last night, so I thought I'd see what the joke was about."

He gave me a wry smile, which I returned. I had no idea I'd been laughing like a crazy person in the middle of the tornado. Without the compassion of my Staff Sergeant, I may not have survived that night.

Staff Var Tui Tui then called out to the group, "Get your kit together. We're heading back to camp. The U.S. Marines have just gone into Kuwait."

It was February 1991.

The big Desert Storm, on the other side of the world, was about to begin.

1: Respect

"Wherever you go, go with all your heart."

—Confucius

I was pushed out of a hovering Bell UH-1 "Huey" Iroquois helicopter. I landed with a thud. A pack was thrown at me, and I looked around to get some semblance of where I was. The view was spectacular but ominous. I was somewhere in the Southern Alps, and I knew I was going to be on my own for the next few days.

The Huey spiraled up into the air and headed off. Dark clouds were rolling in to the south, so I knew that rain was coming before nightfall. Water wasn't going to be an immediate concern, but I needed to make a shelter. I was wearing my flying overalls, and I had my standard-issue knife. The pack contained a parachute and a one-day ration pack, so I'd be okay for the next twenty-four hours. It was clear to me that I needed to move fast and I needed to respect the environment.

New Zealand is a pristine country with a breathtaking wilderness. In the Southern Alps, mountain peaks gaze down onto the forest flora and fauna. There are no predatory animals or poisonous snakes to be concerned with. The weather, however, can kill you. Getting wet and cold is a recipe for disaster, so I quickly strung up a hammock between two suitable trees and used the rest of the parachute to create cover. It would be cold but dry. I took off my boots and used them as a pillow. The rain began as the sun set, and my shelter held up. The quiet rhythm of the rain was calming, and I drifted off to sleep.

I was woken by a pair of moreporks (or "rurus") sometime in the middle of the night. The rain had stopped. Moreporks are large owls. Moreporks make a two-syllable hoot that literally sounds like, "More pork." These two owls had decided to have a long, one-worded conversation. One of them sat on a branch directly above me. The other was somewhere off in the distance. They kept it up for a good hour, most likely discussing the new resident in their otherwise private world.

As I tried to drift back to sleep, I suddenly thought about how I was going to make fire. That, and the moreporks, kept me up for most of the night.

Respect is something we give.

The simple act of paying attention shows respect. Being in the moment shows respect to yourself and all around you. The most respectful thing we can do is to listen to somebody with our undivided attention. To commit to being aware of someone else's feelings and to really concentrate on what someone else is saying takes practice and discipline. It is not easy. Every time we try a little harder to understand someone else better, we are walking the bushido path. It has been said that attention is the rarest and purest form of generosity.

We are taught from an early age to express ourselves better and to develop our communication skills. This is focused largely on talking and writing and "telling" rather than listening and understanding. I am guilty of this lack of listening. I usually have so much going on in my head (that I want to share) that, as a result, I miss the opportunity to listen to others. When we seek to understand rather than to be understood, we create trust through this respect for the other person. We are all ignorant of many things, so to become wiser we need to seek out those areas where we can gain better understanding. We should proactively want to listen and learn as a result. We already know what we know, so we need to listen to others, if we are to learn more about them.

When we step onto the dojo floor, we bow to the Shinzen and say, "Osu." This is respect for the dojo but also respect for the time we are committing to learn. We don't go to the dojo to show off what we know or to demonstrate our prowess. We go to the dojo to learn. We are there to train. We are there to listen. If we are consumed with our own ego and sense of mastery, we will miss the many lessons that will be presented for us to learn in that class or in that training session… even if we are teaching that class. Everyone you meet is your teacher. We all have something to learn from every interaction we have, if we just have the respect to pay attention to the lesson.

It is dojo custom that when you hand something to somebody or receive something from somebody, you use both hands. Using both hands shows that you harbor no ill-will and that you hold no weapon. This simple discipline was taught to me by Kaicho and serves to treat any occasion with a certain degree of reverence and respect. The entire Japanese tea ceremony revolves around a focused respect and appreciation for the moment. When we take time to absorb the moment and appreciate those people and things that surround us, we show respect. The moment then gains more meaning and significance.

One of Kaicho's meditation lectures is a reflection on a very old Judo expression, "Rei Ni Hajimari, Rei Ni Owaru." This means to bow at the start of training and to bow at the end of training. Everything is started "Hajimari" and finished "Owaru" with a bow. When we look at this expression, we see respect being consciously applied to a training environment. When we walk into the dojo, we face the "Shinzen" (a focal point of reverence at the front of the dojo) and bow with a loud, "Osu," to show that we are ready to train. At the end of class, when we step off the dojo floor, we face the Shinzen again and bow with a loud, "Osu," to show that we have concluded our training for the moment.

Kaicho encourages us to start and finish everything we do in life with the same attitude. When we set out to do something, we gain a greater degree of clarity if we pause for a minute to breathe and take stock of the situation. This is "Rei Ni Hajimari" and defines our intention to do something with respect toward the work that is required. When we finish something, we pause to take stock of what has been done. This is "Rei Ni Owaru" and shows respect and appreciation for the work that has been completed—even if there's more work to be done for a larger project. Without becoming conceited, it's important for all of us to recognize what we have done to represent our best selves and continue to follow this path.

The simple application of this principle is to take a breath and internally "bow" before starting something. It could be making a sandwich or mowing the lawn. When we start with an intention to do our best, the work gains more meaning, and we are no longer just going through the motions. When the job is done, take a breath and internally "bow" to acknowledge the completion of what you set out to do.

Take a minute to imagine the effect on the very simple act of making someone a sandwich. If you do this simple job from start to finish, with respect for both the task and recipient, chances are you'll carefully consider the ingredients more thoughtfully, make the sandwich to their liking, and your presentation will be neater and more pleasing to the person you're serving. Who doesn't want to have a sandwich made for them like that? You can become the bushido sandwich maker today! Just pause and add a layer of respect to the ingredients.

When we pause, for even a split second, to consider how we should respond to somebody, we ultimately make a better choice than when we talk first and think later. This respect for others goes beyond what we say and enables us to listen better and respond once we understand the other person's position or point of view in greater detail. We have all seen the reality of confidence being silent and insecurity being loud. It is easier for us to see this in others than to be self-aware enough to observe this in ourselves. We are so busy trying to get our own point across that we often miss out on essential information that we can only obtain through good questions and astute listening.

To respect someone means to care enough to deeply admire them. To admire someone, we must know what their unique qualities and abilities are. To know these unique qualities and abilities, we need to ask questions and listen. Respect comes from knowing somebody and gaining a special insight into their character and spirit. Respect is something we give, not something we get. To ask or expect someone to deeply admire us without bothering to respect that person beforehand is pure vanity. I know this, because I've been guilty of it. Respect is an outward emotion and acknowledgement, not an inward reward from others.

If somebody does have genuine respect for us, we should humbly return that respect and work hard to know that person better. Someone who truly respects us is a precious jewel in our life. When we truly respect someone, we are a precious jewel in that person's life. Such is the rare nature of respect. Respect requires an openness in communication and a degree of vulnerability to allow someone to understand somebody else on a deeper level. When we respect someone, we also appreciate that they have had the courage to open their heart to us and show their true identity. Anything less than this is not true respect, but rather a kind of sycophantic obsequiousness or idolization to gain favor or advantage. The other feeling often confused with respect is fear.

Fear keeps us from stepping forward into the world with an open heart. Think about the ocean. We should all respect the ocean because it is vast and powerful and beautiful. We admire the ocean because in many ways it is beyond our comprehension, and we can never fully understand the depth and mood of the sea. We should not fear the ocean. We should learn more about the sea, so we know where it is safe to swim and where it is dangerous. This is the difference between respect and fear. Fear will hold us back from enjoying the wonderful bounty of the ocean. Respect will allow us to appreciate the ocean in more detail. When we respect something or someone, we no longer have to embrace fear.

In both our private and professional lives, we often find ourselves looking for the respect of others. This is a mistake. We assume too much of others when we seek respect, and we forget that respect is our responsibility to give, rather than ours to receive. This sounds like a very simple concept, but our ego does not like this whole idea of giving something we shouldn't receive back in return. The ego doesn't like this, because the ego is insecure. Throw away your ego. Let go of the drive for self-promotion to appease other people and to "big" yourself up. Nobody truly respects anybody, unless they take the time to see the pure intentions within their heart. So, seeking respect is simply a waste of time and a waste of your precious life.

In the business world, a degree of knowledge, skill, and experience is essential to command the attention of colleagues and clients. It is easy to fall into the trap of assuming a superior role and the "upper hand" in a competitive environment. Again, this is the insecure ego. The secret to developing respect for others is to ask the right questions and then listen. Seek clarification if the answer doesn't make sense. When the intention is to build respect, the results follow naturally. How many people do you interact with who ask pertinent, considered questions about what it is you need? If you're lucky enough to have these people in your life, the chances are you are a very loyal customer.

Businesses often talk about a "competitive edge" to differentiate themselves from other organizations in the same field. Advertising often addresses this with a lot of chest-pumping, self-congratulatory mumbo jumbo, followed by a very negative overview of the competition. The same is true of modern politics. The irony with this bushido focus on building respect for others (rather than gaining respect) is that it shies away from self-promotion and steadily looks toward building trust and appreciation for empathy. Businesses and politicians cannot buy this trust or respect. Our very motivation to want to understand better and respect more will become our competitive edge.

At home, we share a complex history with our family. When we are determined to be heard and understood, we often find we get more and more frustrated, because we just can't get our point across. They (family members) just don't understand what we're going through, and we feel hurt that they just don't get it. This is pure ego. When we have enough determination to develop our respect for someone, we listen.

Don't get me wrong: I'm not saying this is easy. This is bushido training, after all. If it were easy, everyone would be doing it! But seriously, we have the ability to develop that respect for others when we seek to understand rather than be understood. If you apply this respect (completely, not partially) with someone with whom you often have communication challenges, you'll see a positive change.

Teenagers, in particular, want (and need) to be heard. They've heard the rules a million times, and they don't necessarily need to be reminded of them. They don't need to hear how easy they have it and how tough it was for us, "back in the day," when things weren't so cushy and comfortable. Teenagers need our respect. This is a particularly hard challenge for all of us (when teaching or just dealing with teenagers), because we see the lessons to be learned and we have the experience to make good suggestions for them. We often assume too much about what the teenager is currently going through. The best solution to clarify this is to ask questions. The fact that teenagers don't always provide direct answers to direct questions shouldn't deter us from seeking to understand. It takes patience.

The interrelationship between the eight principles of the samurai become very clear as we diligently continue to examine the disciplines required to execute these virtues in our daily life. Respect takes courage and compassion. Respect seeks the truth and desires justice for others. Respect honors others and confirms loyalty. Respect, most of all, requires self-control, because we so often want to be understood before we are open to understand. We assume we have all the answers when we clearly do not. Respect is about our willingness to accept our ignorance and seek to do something about that by learning how to admire someone else through knowledge.

Respect enables us to step out of the darkness of self-absorption and into the light of empathy. We move beyond our own self-made complications (and the associated depression and anxiety) when we focus on understanding others. Delight is the reward for those who pay attention. When we learn through seeking the truth, we feel happier and more centered, as a result. This is the beauty of developing and giving respect.

When Kaicho created Seido Karate in 1976, his philosophy was encapsulated in three words: Love, Respect, Obedience. Love is fundamental to developing respect for others with an obedient mind that doesn't settle for a poor effort. Respect is the cornerstone of Kaicho's philosophy and is reflected in the way he teaches. Kaicho instructs with such an open heart and with so much care and attention to his students, you can feel Kaicho's respect for all of his students. This creates a class full of love, respect, and obedience. As students, we all respect Kaicho for this.

We are often reminded by Kaicho to remember our role in setting and maintaining standards in the dojo. If you are a black belt, you should behave like someone who has been training for more than five years, and you should set an example in terms of behavior, deportment, etiquette, and effort. This shows respect for what the belt/rank represents rather than an ego driven desire to strut about as a "senior" student. The senior students we most respect are friendly but respectful and carry themselves with a considered understanding of their role in the dojo, which includes cleaning the floor, the mirrors, and the locker room. The senior students who have most clearly grasped the essence of Seido Karate are those who serve the dojo most.

Applying this attitude of respect and service to life outside of the dojo can be difficult. Try it. When somebody is about to give a presentation or make an announcement at work, fetch them a glass of water. This is not subservience or "sucking up" or demeaning; it is respectful and kind. It takes no effort other than the desire to be respectful.

The same is true whenever we walk into a new environment that we're unsure of. Show it respect. Treat every new place you visit like a dojo, and you'll be surprised at how people will appreciate that. Once that habit is established, find new ways to appreciate places you're very familiar with. You'll be well on your way down the path of respect.

A traditional Japanese bow shows respect without any words needing to be said. The same is true of a respectful tip of the hat, a salute, or showing appreciation by bringing your open palms together. These body language "signs" all communicate respect and appreciation and are easily incorporated into everyday life.

When thanking someone, I always try to face them (head on) and look them in the eye. If the person I'm thanking is a martial artist (or Japanese), I bow out of sheer habit. I find, when I am touched by something very kind, bringing my palms together not only shows my heightened gratitude, but it also helps to settle me a little, so I can compose myself better to respond. These are bushido techniques used to express love and respect.

If we sincerely wish to make a positive impact on the world around us, respect is an essential part of that mission. Searching for and finding ways to admire more about people and the world around us will automatically make us more present and more aware of our surroundings. When we are more present, we are naturally happier, because we are living in the "now" rather than the past or future. Respect gives the happy samurai a reason to smile.

Back in the Southern Alps, I woke to start my first day of my three-day survival training. I fashioned a walking stick, ate a rock-hard biscuit from my ration pack, and followed the natural topography of the immediate area to find some water.

I found a small stream and drank thirstily. The ground was wet, and I had little faith in my ability to use the bow-drill or hand-drill method to start a fire. I then spotted a longfin eel drifting beneath the bank of the stream. I checked my ration pack to see what I could possibly eat with eel.

I then discovered a pack of waterproof matches in the ration pack. Of course, I'd been told matches were in the ration pack, but I'd forgotten. I knew I'd be okay.

The next three days were challenging but excellent survival training. Some common sense and an appreciation and respect for Mother Nature made it an experience I will always treasure. The eel was delicious.

1: Sincerity

"To thine own self be true."

—William Shakespeare

My escape route had inexplicably closed off behind me. Alone in the cockpit of my CT/4 Airtrainer, I scanned the horizon for a break in the clouds that formed a solid blanket, 2,000 feet below me. I had less than 100 hours of flying experience in my Air Force log book. I was rated for visual flight rules (VFR), but I was not rated for instrument flight rules (IFR). Flying into the clouds below me was not an option. I was on a solo cross-country navigation exercise, and two of my course mates had already made precautionary landings at civilian airports because of the weather. A few had already returned to the exercise's base in Rotorua. I had plenty of fuel, but I was in a pickle. Any sort of engine problem would spell disaster.

My flight instructor had taught me the basics of instrument flying, but I had no experience flying IFR solo, and I wasn't rated to do so. I'd be effectively breaking the law and risking my life, if I decided to descend into the clouds.

I knew where I was, but I had no visible clues below me to help me navigate. I made a decision to set a course for the last point of my prescribed navigation route. I'd fly there and then circle the area and hopefully find a break in the clouds, so I could descend back into Rotorua and land.

I could still potentially finish my navigation circuit and land within the time frame that we needed to adhere to. I could still "win" the course navigation competition. But how would I eventually explain how I managed to do this?

The truth is not for everyone. The truth takes courage, because it can be frightening and can take us out of the relative safety and comfort of ignorance or delusion. "Ignorance is bliss." is something we can all relate to, but can this really be associated with happiness? Being high on heroin may be blissful, but it is not living in reality. Truth is often a tough pill to swallow, because it can prove to us that we are ignorant or wrong about something. The ego hates to be wrong!

When I started Seido Karate in 1996, I thought the word "Seido," which means "sincere way," was an unusual name for a style of martial arts. It didn't sound strong or tough or frightening to me. Such was my ignorance of the true nature of bushido. Sincerity is one of the hardest and most challenging disciplines of all, because it cannot be achieved only in part; it must be embraced as a constant endeavor. You can't be "sort of sincere" or partially true. Seido Karate fosters a desire to be true to oneself and true to the world we live in.

This "sincere way" of Seido Karate acknowledges a path and a journey rather than a destination. It's not "truth at the top of the mountain," but a training program to develop the mind, body, and spirit in a continuous commitment to the way of sincerity. This is the heart of bushido and takes both courage and discipline. Face the truth. Acknowledge the truth. Walk through the truth, and live with it in your life. The alternative is delusion, so we may as well take truth anyway. Like the blue pill or the red pill in the movie, *The Matrix*, we all have a choice to face reality or shy away from it out of fear.

I have mentioned "Shoshin," which means "beginner's mind." This is a concept that needs complete sincerity, if the true value of the lesson is to be learned and experienced. A beginner's mind sincerely wants to learn something new. It's not about putting on a show and "looking" like you want to learn something new; rather, it's a sincere desire to listen and learn. This takes practice. From time to time, Kaicho has invited his Kodokan friend, (Shihan) Yoichiro Matsumura, to teach a judo seminar at Honbu. I find these types of experiences to be so rewarding, as the ego is thrown away as fast as my feet are swept away. This sincere attitude toward training should not be reserved for such occasions, but instead applied to all classes and to life in general.

Children are our greatest teachers when it comes to sincerity. Children are, by nature, honest and sincere until they learn how to be otherwise (usually by observing adults). Children's capacity to learn languages, play music, sing, dance, and create are all driven by a sincere desire to learn. Adults do not lack the brain capacity to learn these things, but they lack the sincere attitude to embrace the unknown. Yes, we're all a lot busier than children, with our work and other responsibilities, but that's a ready excuse. It's our ego that doesn't want to address ignorance of a topic or a lack of knowledge about something. The ego gets in our way of learning new things.

When children compete at karate tournaments, I am always amazed at how sincerely they perform, when doing kata. They try their hardest but don't beat themselves up, if they make a mistake. I have seen this time and time again. When a child makes a mistake in a kata, they will usually just start again and give it their best sincere effort. No drama. No frustration. They just get on with it.

Not so much with adults! Adults tend to get frustrated and angry with themselves and lose focus, composure, and balance as a result. I know this from personal experience, so I'm not giving anyone a hard time here. Try playing golf with adults and children, and observe the difference in attitude. Children approach life with a sincere heart. This is something to emulate and learn from.

How do we build on a journey that accommodates a sincere way? To start with, we need to back ourselves and know that we can do it. We need to tell our ego to be quiet and reflect on our ability to be self-aware and honest with ourselves. If you're reading this book, you're already there (on the road), because you're seeking knowledge and you want to be a happier samurai. The road is already there for you, so all you need to do is continue on your journey.

So, how do we get started on this "sincere way" path? And how do we stay on this journey and get stronger and stronger (and happier and happier) in the process?

The first step of any journey is just that: the first step. Once the first step has been taken, we continue to practice, and the journey becomes ours and ours alone. If you get off track, just stop and start again. Your sincere way will be a unique and special journey that you and you alone will navigate. I recall a quote from the Buddha, "Each morning we are born again. What we do today is what matters most." The time to start is now, because today is your day to shine. No other time currently exists.

The Japanese word "makoto" means "truthfulness," and this applies to what we say as well as to what we do. In everything we do, Seido Karate students aspire to develop a sincere, honest straightforwardness. The benefits of this "truthfulness" at home, at work, and in the world are enormous. Life becomes less complicated and fractious, when we are not hiding or evading but are being open and honest.

Think of how rare it is to know someone whom you completely trust. Only a history of sincerity can create trust. In the business world, corporations often talk about "scaling" a product or service to reach a larger audience and exponentially grow the enterprise as a result. The problem with this theory (when you are involved in businesses that require trust and honesty) is the fact that you simply cannot scale trust—it is that rare. Most corporations don't have the time or energy to invest in creating real trust, so they often resort to the kind of trite obfuscation we're all well aware of. It is so easy to see right through that kind of insincerity.

At home, trust is a reaffirmation of the strength and reliability of those members in the family. The love we have for our family members is deepened by the trust we share and the myriad experiences we have had to reinforce that trust. There is no need to be anything but completely sincere with our family, because they know

LUKE MAYES

us so well and can see right through any attempt to cloud the truth. Family is so important because the years deliver the truth in all things, and we often know our family members longer than anyone else we will ever know.

There is a beautiful Japanese saying that Kaicho often talks about in meditation class, "Mukei zaisan shinyo." This means, "Invisible treasure—trust," and reflects on the richness and value of things that are invisible (trust) but felt at the very bottom of our hearts. Trust is something invisible and precious. There is no fast track to earning someone's trust. It is the result of many occasions and experiences when that trust is reaffirmed through actions rather than words. Trust cannot be bought at any price, so it is a priceless treasure that makes our very soul rich and prosperous. The "wealthiest" people in the world have very little, if they cannot trust anyone. This feeling of non-trust is the polar opposite of happiness.

Trust is created through truth, respect, honor, love, integrity, and kindness—all the virtues fostered through the tenets of the samurai. Friends whom you trust are dear and valued. To earn trust, we must look after people with a sincere heart. We must prove that we are reliable and dependable; we don't get to set the timetable on when that trust will be acquired. Think of someone whom you truly trust and someone who trusts you. It has taken years to develop this wondrous thing called trust, which has been built on the years of honesty between you. Rightly or wrongly, a betrayal of that trust wipes the slate clean, and the trust must be built again and earned again from scratch. Such is the precious nature of trust.

Our ego needs to come to terms with the reality that we are far better and more perfect than we think we are (when insecurely comparing ourselves to other people), but also not as "important" as we think we are (when insecurely pumping ourselves up with untruths and false bravado). We live in a world where ego-driven self-promotion has become a very normal thing. We exaggerate our accomplishments or bend the truth to make ourselves feel "big" or more important. Most of us are guilty of this, because, through osmosis, we fall into this trap of self-doubt. The truth is we don't fool anyone but ourselves with insincere self-promotion. Nobody is impressed with insecure boasting. If we don't back up our words with consistent actions, we are nothing but noise.

"Fugen Jikko" means "Act without words," and this is the essence of Kaicho's philosophy, when it comes to developing a sincere way through Seido Karate training. Don't talk about it, just get on with it. Show your sincerity through your actions rather than tell everyone about it.

Whenever we just "do" something sincere and honest, we feel a deep sense of balance and alignment with our best self. Nobody else needs to know about it, because we know it in our hearts. A dollar to a homeless person or helping someone cross the street or just saying hello to a stranger with a smile—these are kind and sincere actions that build a stronger heart and a happier samurai. Those closest to us will see the difference in us, because we will be less eager to "prove" who we are as a result of just "being" who we are.

We cannot escape the truth. We might try. We might fool ourselves that we don't actually need to be completely honest about certain things. We can rationalize, but we'll still have to face the truth in the end. Truth is the daughter of time. When we are not in line with our true selves, we create disorder in our lives, which can manifest in our relationships with others, as well as in our own internal health. When we are sincere, our relationships with others prosper and deepen, and our internal health is more likely to flourish and thrive, as a result.

Notwithstanding the fact that deceit and lies carry the burden of cross-referencing with even more lies, as well as the stress and anxiety of employing reluctant corroborators, it's not a happy (or healthy) way to live. Think of the last time you "came clean" with someone you care about. How good did that feel? The temporary challenge of dealing with the consequences (if any) soon evaporates as you gain trust and no longer need to be anxious about covering tracks and adding to the pile of deception.

We live in a world with stress and drama, so we don't need to actively add stress and drama into our lives by being insincere. When we are sincere, we remove stress and drama from our lives and become more at ease; as a result, less "dis-ease" will manifest. Simply put, honesty is good for your health and makes you happy. The truth shall set you free.

We don't want to hurt people with "truths" that are unkind, but we do want to be honest and open. Respect, as we have examined, often requires well-thought-out questions and an earnest desire to find the truth. When we ask questions and give our full attention to the answers, we are seeking the truth rather than our preconceived version of the truth. We might think someone has a fault or a character trait that is not positive. When we spend the time asking questions to discover what might be behind those character traits, we have the opportunity to find out more about the person and where we stand with them. The mutual trust develops as a result.

An easy test we can apply to any relationship we have is to ask the question, "Is this relationship simple and truthful now?" If not, we have a responsibility to work on improving that dynamic with our own honesty. The onus is on us rather than "them," because we can only control our own ability to be sincere. What we do is more important than what we say, but what we say is still critical. Before we speak, we should quickly filter the language between our brain and our mouth. Socrates said we should ask this question (of ourselves) before speaking, "Is it true, is it kind, or is it necessary?"

We have a limited time to enjoy and appreciate the experience of life, so wasting our time on false realities and deceit dishonors our very existence. Kaicho's book, *One Day, One Lifetime,* covers many of his meditation lectures and reinforces the need to approach life with a sincere heart. Each day, we start anew. This is our life. Yesterday is gone, so we move forward and embrace the present. We all have the opportunity to gain a heightened sense of dignity and self-respect by approaching the world with a sincere heart. This is the noble philosophy of Seido Karate and can be applied to everyone's life. Do justice to your life.

One of the hardest challenges we face in life is the development of sincere self-awareness. We know how easy it is to be "objective" about other people, but not so much when it comes to addressing our own objectivity. As we become increasingly sincere toward others, we have a better opportunity to observe and understand our own behavior and actions. When we question what our motivations are, we can then channel our energy into those activities that are best in line with our mission or sense of purpose. If we do something for money, we understand that, but if we do something for an honest desire to benefit others, there is an energy and drive that surpasses our efforts when they are motivated solely by financial gain.

The word "amateur" is used to describe someone who engages in an activity or sport on an unpaid (rather than professional) basis. The word is derived from the Latin word "amator," which means "lover." I have taught karate as a professional, and I have taught karate as an amateur. It makes no difference to the energy I put into the class. Why? Because I love it! When you find those things that you naturally pursue as an "amateur," you are driven by a motivation that will carry you beyond your capacity as a "professional," because your sincere love for what you do will create an added magic—the magic of sincere joy.

Professional athletes often fall into the money trap, snared by agents and managers. They are pushed to make more and more money, and you can observe that they often look less and less passionate about their sport, because they have become more professional than amateur. We have all seen this time and time again in many different sporting arenas.

Money is necessary. We all need to make money, but a sincere heart will recognize what we love and what is important to us. This is the jewel of our individual talent. It can be walking dogs, teaching kids, coaching soccer, feeding homeless people, or any number of activities that bring our talent and passion to the table in the service of others. This is the sincere way.

Seeking the truth when we risk being wrong, as a result, is a sure sign of wisdom. If we are to learn, we must accept that we don't have all the answers, and we also have some of the answers wrong. Having friends who can be frank and honest when asked for advice is a priceless gift. When we can return the favor with a sincere heart, those friendships deepen and become more and more enriched as a result. Honesty between friends builds a grounded house of stability and love that can weather the harshest storms. Sincerity builds a strong support system and the warm feeling of interdependence.

As a karate instructor, I encourage students in different ways, depending on what motivates the individual. I always try to be as honest as I can be and focus on areas that can be improved upon. Kaicho creates an environment where your best will always be good enough, but it has to be your best. Following Kaicho's example, I push the physically gifted students very hard, while trying to find the greatest "strength" and "weakness" in each individual, so there is always a benchmark for measuring performance and improvement. I want my students to compete with themselves based on their capacity. It's always useful to be able to praise someone (when improving) or note that they are capable of more (when slacking).

(Sei Shihan) Debra Hershkowitz is a senior instructor at Honbu in New York. Whenever I am preparing for a tournament, I will perform katas in front of Sei Shihan, to get her feedback. She will not allow me to get away with anything less than what she sees as my best effort. She will be absolutely honest with her assessment of my technique, deportment, posture, stances, focus, speed, transitions, pacing, and every other aspect of the kata. She is not concerned with my ego, and this is what makes this kind of assessment so real and valuable.

You cannot improve without this type of conscientious objectivity. I am so grateful for this, because so few people can really look closely at the nuance of each move without forgetting the basics. Kaicho and Nidaime are both gifted in this area of observance across all facets of training, because they spend so much time paying close attention. I am still a humble student in this department and recognize that I need to keep working on this aspect of my teaching, particularly in regard to kata. Authentic sincerity, like all of the tenets, takes practice.

Our capacity to take and benefit from constructive criticism is directly proportional to our own ability to be honest with others. When we have a sincere heart, our ability to be open and trusting is enhanced, and that can make us more vulnerable. We know that vulnerability takes courage, so honesty creates and nurtures courage. If our trust is betrayed or not reciprocated, this is not our "water to carry," and we don't need to be hurt by this. We choose our own path, not the path of others.

We often see cynical people who behave as if they do not trust anyone or as though everyone is against them. These cynical people see the reflection of their own heart, which is a heart that needs more sincerity. What we focus on gets bigger in our perception of the world, so, if we are open to honesty, we will find it. If we are not open to honesty, we cannot find it, because it doesn't exist for us.

We do not "lose" when we are honest or when we seek the truth. We become wiser and more centered. The political and corporate arena would suggest otherwise.

When we are surrounded by dishonesty and fact-bending, we can feel like that's just the way life is. It is true that life exists for many people who believe "winning" is more important than "reality"; these people live in a world of their own making. Observe how threatened some people become when faced with truth. They may well be terrified of truth, because it flies in the face of their own make-believe reality. This is not a happy existence. This is delusion and will create a constant lack of connectedness and greater insecurity.

When we observe this incredible world we all live in and seek the meaning and truth behind our own existence, we are living a life that is worthy and sublime. The delight and bliss that come from discovering life's truths are far beyond any material possession that can be gained through dishonesty or subterfuge. The happy samurai observes a world that is complex and layered but simple and can be connected to through the development of a sincere heart. What we feel and experience in life has far more value than the ownership of objects. Think about times that have made you feel proud and "in the right place" and special (in a non-ego way), and you'll discover that these feelings came from being in the present moment as your most authentic self.

Acquiring a house or a car or getting a job can feel amazing. When we achieve these things through our own efforts, we feel a sense of accomplishment. As long as we don't dwell on self-congratulation, these things should be celebrated and appreciated.

The maturing of our self-awareness will allow us to observe what our motivations were behind these accomplishments. Recognizing these motivations is how we become more in tune with who we really are and what we are capable of. The achievements of a sincere heart have no repercussions or guilt associated with them. The benefits of sincerity are pure and simple and noble.

###

When I reached the final location point of my cross-country navigation route, I began to circle my Airtrainer. I needed to calculate when I should start my final leg, so I could land on time and "win" the exercise. The instructors were taking bets on the students, so my instructor would also "win," and we'd both have bragging rights among our respective peers.

I no longer needed to consider an IFR approach as the clouds had started to clear. If the clouds started to thicken again, I would abandon the mission and just get the aircraft below the cloud base and land. My "mental dead reckoning" complete, I started the last leg and finished with a direct landing approach to touch down within ten seconds of my "wheels down" target time.

I taxied off the airstrip and was met by my instructor, (Flight Lieutenant) Ian "Wallsy" Walls. Wallsy looked concerned. Wallsy was an ex-A-4 Skyhawk pilot and didn't suffer fools gladly.

I shut down the aircraft and popped open the Airtrainer's canopy. I busied myself with my helmet and maps.

"Ten seconds! How did you manage that?" Wallsy asked.

I could see the concern and empathy in his eyes. He knew that I wasn't IFR-rated and knew what I'd just been through.

I took a deep breath and fessed up to the fact that I'd gone directly to the last marker point, once I'd found myself above the cloud base. He smiled and told me that we would forfeit. We both learned a lot about each other in that moment.

1: Honor

"Gratitude for your parents should be higher than the mountain, deeper than the sea."

—Kaicho Nakamura

The soldier's head had stopped bleeding. Thankfully, the wound was superficial. His heart was beating after the CPR I'd administered earlier.

We rattled about in the back of a big Unimog Army truck as it bumped along a muddy, heavily rutted road. I had laid the soldier on one of the two side benches and knelt in front of him, checking for respiration. He'd stopped breathing again. I started mouth to mouth resuscitation. *Why didn't we have a proper medic with us?*

As the platoon commander, I should have delegated this, but I felt responsible. The rest of the platoon would sort themselves out under the supervision of the platoon sergeant. We were about fifteen minutes from camp, so I just needed to keep this soldier breathing. The other soldier in the back of the truck looked on, ready to help if needed. I thought about my parents.

We all have different relationships with our parents. If not for our parents, we would not exist, so we must always be grateful for our parents and honor them.

Of my mother's many lessons to me, "Everything is a matter of perspective," is one I hold dearest. As a "know-it-all" teenager, I used to roll my eyes at my mother's various philosophical revelations, but they have made more and more sense and become more and more relevant as I have grown older. Listen to your mother! We all have the opportunity to view the world as we see fit. Our perspective is something we have the ability to control, however hard this can be to realize.

We can choose to see something like a meal with a parent as normal and mundane. We can choose to see a meal with a parent as special and meaningful. What we bring to the table makes the difference in what we see and how we feel. When we honor someone (or something), we give them (or it) dignity, and we respect the inherent integrity we recognize and admire. That's not to say that we think our parents are perfect. Far from it. Like us, our parents are beautifully flawed and human. Like us, our parents have strengths and weaknesses. When we focus on the weaknesses of anyone, we find it difficult to honor and respect them. When we focus on the strengths of anyone, we find it easy to admire them and clearly see their integrity and dignity. This is a choice we make about how we view our parents.

"Oya no On," means, "Parents should be shown appreciation." The Japanese character "*oya*" for "parents" is made up of three characters: to "stand" in a "tree" and "look out" (for the children). We must show gratitude for the many times our parents have looked out for us…, even when we were not aware of it. We cannot remember the stress and love and dedication of our parents when we were little babies, so we should take time to think about that and appreciate and honor the fact that our parents brought us into the world.

Honor requires us to pause and take time to appreciate. When we take the time to examine something in more detail, we can develop a reverence and a sense of awe. Awe is a powerful feeling, because it is something beyond our own ego. When we are in awe, we are completely present in the world around us, and we cannot feel depression or anxiety at that very moment. A happy samurai is in awe of the world and the people in it. Perspective allows us to view what we choose to view (positive or negative); the perspective and energy we choose will resonate with everything in the world around us.

We can "love" our car or "hate" our car. We can "love" our job or "hate" our job. What we esteem and honor takes on value and makes us feel rich and blessed. There are always positive aspects of a car or a job. What we negate and dishonor becomes a negative burden and makes us feel poor and victimized. There are always negative aspects of a car or job. While we accept challenges and take on burdens, it is a gift for us to develop a positive outlook on all that we experience in life, even when we grieve the death of someone close.

Grief is an absolutely essential part of life (and processing) and cannot be ignored, but this is balanced with a positive reflection of what was so beautiful about that person, when they were alive or with us. If they weren't beautiful humans in some way, we wouldn't grieve. The tears we shed yesterday should water the seeds of growth we plant for our future.

Another classic from my mother is, "What doesn't kill us makes us stronger." I don't credit my mother for creating this saying, but she may have actually said this more than anyone in history! As I reflect back on the myriad times my mother said this to me, I think of how very "bushido" this expression is. It honors our mistakes and our pitfalls. It takes into account that you either succeed or learn. When you "lose" (and don't die in the process), you learn and get stronger and often become more adroit, as a result. There's no losing when you adopt this mentality. You just keep carrying on, knowing that you're building experience and knowledge all the time.

My parents taught me a lot about honor. My father was a very honorable man. I learned a lot about life from observing my father. I remember playing tennis against a kid when I was about nine years old, and the kid was better than me. My father was watching. As it became apparent that the kid was going to beat me, I faked an injury and started limping about the place.

When the game was over, my father asked if I was really hurt. He looked me in the eye. I started to cry with shame. My father put his arm around me and said, "Don't take the victory away from your opponent." That lesson has stuck with me ever since, and I have always remembered to honor people against whom I have competed—win or lose.

We must learn to honor ourselves before we can truly honor others. We need to make this a habit, in order to establish an appreciation for how honor can work in our lives. My nine-year-old ego didn't allow me to honor my opponent on the tennis court all those years ago, but the lesson still stands today in any situation where my ego is easily bruised or threatened. I often ask myself, "What would a wise person do right now?" This confronts my "know-it-all" ego and asks me to honor my best self in any given situation.

Honor and respect are very similar concept, and both are used to reflect an admiration of someone or something. We honor someone with respect. The traditions of honor in a samurai's life go further still. If a warrior was defeated in battle and lost his honor, he would commit the ritual "seppuku" (suicide with a sword) and leave the world in disgrace. Our modern interpretation of honor might not be so extreme, but we can admire the commitment in the samurai's life to maintaining honor and the principals of etiquette.

Japan in the Edo era (1603-1868) was relatively peaceful. The samurai during this time were permitted to carry two swords (a katana and a shorter wakizashi), which was an important symbol of their authority. It was forbidden for samurai to draw their sword, but they were allowed to use their sword to protect their honor. If a samurai drew his sword, he meant business. Even if the blade was drawn just "three sun out" (or about four inches out) of the sheath, a samurai could turn his entire family into "ronin" for all future generations. To become "ronin" would dishonor the family and take away all status and recognition as descendants of samurai. There is something beautiful and honorable about this code of conduct.

For a samurai, no idle threat (or promise) is not honored. When we bark threats and don't back them up, we are like a yapping dog with no bite. When we make promises and don't follow through, we are worse still. Without honoring our words with deeds, we gain no respect from the world we live in. Conversely, when we honor our words with action, we not only show respect for our own honor, but we gain the respect and trust of those around us. For the happy samurai in the modern world, honor is about our dedication to doing what we say and saying what we do... or keeping our mouths closed!

When a karateka is awarded a black belt, the training really begins. Like a university graduate, a new black belt has learned the basics and now has to apply those basics to become a more rounded human. I do not blame or belittle people who earn a black belt and then decide to quit training. I just feel bad for them. I feel sorry that they are missing out on what I see as the best part of karate-do training. They miss out on the day-to-day polishing of technique they already know, to keep working on techniques and sculpt them into their own art. I hope they all honor their training by continuing on in their lives as better humans for having studied a martial art. The wonderful thing about Seido Karate-do is the fact that the door is always open for returning students.

I used to wear a Seido tracksuit jacket over my gi at open karate tournaments. I remember feeling I always needed to honor Kaicho when I was competing, and that jacket represented how I should conduct myself. Whatever I did, however I behaved, the jacket would say I was from Seido Karate, so I needed to keep that in mind and act accordingly. This sounds like such a simple thing, but I actually needed that degree of self-control in those days, so the jacket took the place of what should have been honor for myself. We can often justify what we know is bad behavior, but when we honor something that is outside of ourselves (even a badge or symbol) we can better serve ourselves as a result by keeping our ego in check.

I have talked about respect for seniors in the dojo. As a senior to some and a junior to others, I have a place in the dojo that I must honor. This means I need to clean the floor and pay attention to dojo etiquette because this is my responsibility as a senior. It also means I need to respect and appreciate my seniors who have been training for many years and who have so much to teach me through their example and council. Regardless of "rank" or experience, the dojo is a place we honor each other through correct behavior and a dedication to giving our best. This is not always so serious and not without kindness and humor, but to honor the dojo means to never be offhand or ungracious.

When I moved to California from New York, Nidaime encouraged a large number of students to attend my last fight class and he presented me with a plaque to reflect his appreciation of my 23 years at Honbu. I have taught my own classes and assisted Nidaime for most of this time. It has been an honor for me. When I was presented with the plaque, I was honored and felt humble and very grateful. I was touched. I didn't feel pumped up or arrogant and I recognize this as a change in me. In my younger days, I did not have the maturity to know how to properly accept an accolade or award. When we feel humbled and grateful, we know we are centered and at peace. We are happy. When we feel arrogant we have an exaggerated view of our own self-importance and we are simply insecure and sad.

Our challenge then is to feel this humbleness and gratitude without the need for accolades or recognition from others. To have honor internally manifested in our heart means to walk with a sense of humble awe. Honor allows us to appreciate this gift of life that we have been given to experience and feel humble as a result. Every day we wake up, we are being honored by the universe with our ability to live life and we should return that honor with how we behave in the world we live in. When we honor our own life, we tune in to our most authentic self and reach our highest potential to be happy as a result. The further we are from our true self, the less happy we will be, so honor requires us to respect the truth and embrace it.

Walking an honorable path shows respect for ourselves, our parents, our teachers, our family, our friends and our community. We represent the sum of our life's experience and we have a responsibility to honor that. The challenges we have faced are reflected in our hard work, strength of character and compassion for others. The benefits and privileges we have had are reflected in our gratitude, generosity and kindness. Honor takes on board all of our experiences and transforms these into a grounded reflection of our maturity and capability. As we grow older, we are capable of more because we have more experience to draw from.

Where is happiness? This is a question Kaicho often asks his students to address after meditation class. Everyone has a different version of happiness and different things will make different people happy. We need to honor our own happiness and respect that other people have their own path. Regardless of our unique goals and desires, we often look out to the future for what we perceive to be our happiness when we should be more focused on the present. Kaicho uses the analogy of a lighthouse to explain; even though light is cast 360 degrees and over many miles, there is a blind spot directly below the light in the area closest to the lighthouse.

Like the lighthouse, our vision is often cast off to a place that is far and away from where we are now. We should seek to be happy here and now. We should embrace and enjoy life now. To honor our life, we need to live it and experience it in the only moment we can truly appreciate and experience it - now. Whatever our challenges, we can face them far more effectively if we are present and more grounded. To have big future goals and dreams is a wonderful thing but there is so much to be grateful for in the here and now. If we have our health, a job, people who love us, good friends, a bed to sleep in, food to eat or a view of the sky, we have reason to be happy.

Give honor to your life today. What we do today, creates the potential for tomorrow so the best way to plan for the future is to be truly alive today. When we tune into the world that surrounds us, we have so much more to experience and gain wisdom from. The opposite is true when we tune out and become separate from our present situation. Alcohol, drugs and anything that we think will help us "escape" our reality, will take us further and further away from being present. Even when life is tough and challenging, we honor our own place in it all by the way we address the world and by the way we act.

Different roles that we play in life require different "hats" that define our responsibilities and position. In my mind, I like to replace the figurative hat with an imaginary jacket with the role plastered on the back as big and bold as a gang patch. Just like the Seido jacket, the figurative jacket that represents me being an uncle, brother, son, teacher, student or friend needs to be honored. When I'm wearing that jacket, all that I do should honor the role and the responsibility I take on board to best represent myself in that role. As an uncle, I aim to honor that role by being kind, generous, understanding and empathetic. As a son, I aim to honor that role by being grateful and respectful and obedient. As a brother and as a friend, I aim to honor that role by being considerate, sincere and loyal. Anything we can create to trigger a more honorable approach to our life, in the roles that we play, will make us happier and more fulfilled.

There is an argument that many ranks and titles throughout the martial arts community are superfluous. When badges or stripes or titles give someone a sense of entitlement, they dishonor that title. As a Godan (fifth degree black belt), I am a senior teacher and I am referred to as "Kyoshi" by my fellow kohai. That "title" means that I have a responsibility to know my material and to teach it properly. That is the start and finish of it. I'm no more entitled to anything in the dojo than a brand new white belt walking onto the dojo floor for the first time. My responsibility, to honor my role in the dojo, is to teach that white belt properly and then clean the floor together after class. We both wear white gis and are both students of Seido Karate-do.

Outside of the dojo environment, titles can be less about responsibility and more about "power" and this is where our martial arts training cautions us about dishonoring responsibility by surrendering to our ego. Whatever your various roles are in the world, you do honor to yourself and that "office" or "position" by how you behave and how you commit to those roles, without ego. We all have so much to learn from those we are responsible to teach, manage or take care of. A "rank" carries authority and influence but means nothing if it does not serve the best interests of the role's duty. Nobody's "rank" should be about pompous self-importance because there is nothing to learn or be gained from such a "rank" or title.

When learning a new kata the techniques and "moves" need to be memorized and then melded together. Through repetition the kata doesn't change form, but the expression of the kata evolves as the student no longer worries about remembering the order of the techniques. At this stage, different parts of the kata can be emphasized and nuances in timing can be developed. The original form is honored but the student's own expression or "voice" is also honored within that template. Just like listening to someone sing their version of an old song, it is a beautiful thing to observe a kata that is expressed through the unique capacity of a student's physical ability.

To honor the original form, it is important to teach kata without the addition of too many personal nuances, so the form remains consistent. The kata that I demonstrate when teaching should look a little different from the kata I do on the dojo floor or at a tournament. Like kata, the study and examination of the tenets of the samurai give us a universal template on how to live, but we express this in our own unique way. We are not robots. How you honor your life is entirely up to you, but you should know that you are a special, one-of-a-kind jewel that sparkles and shines like no other jewel in the universe. That is a fact. Honor that.

To honor others with generous gifts makes us more honorable. The most generous gifts are gifts from the heart. One of the most precious gifts we can give someone is trust, because it reflects a period of time when we have appreciated and believed in them. When we listen intently, we honor the person with our focus and attention and learn to trust them more. Even seemingly small gifts can have a massive impact, when they are heartfelt and given with a generous spirit and deep understanding of that person. When we are determined to understand someone better, we honor them. Sometimes, the best present is to simply be present.

Martial arts training can be like moving meditation, when we focus all our energy into trying our best to execute a technique. When we do basic punching, an exercise that is repeated thousands of times throughout our training, we honor the exercise by giving our best effort. One of the best ways to rid the mind of distractions is to do pushups or burpees, to get the heart rate up and the blood flowing. When we start to sweat and feel the physical challenge of training, we are less likely to be distracted, and we can apply more of our focus on the basics. How are we standing? Where are we looking? Are we striking the same target area each time we punch? Is our chamber hand in the right position? Are we striking with the correct part of the fist? Are we keeping our elbows in and rotating the punch at the very last second? Are the fists closed properly? There are many things to think about, even when we have done a technique many times.

At first, we don't know what we don't know. This is unconscious ineptitude. We then become aware of what we don't know. This is conscious ineptitude. I know I can't speak Russian or play the piano. We then develop conscious aptitude. This is when we start training and can remember the various techniques through focus and concentration on what the elements of the technique entail. We then develop unconscious aptitude. This is when we do things automatically and without a lot of figuring out.

The danger in martial arts training (and in life) is to stop at unconscious aptitude. Even with speech and conversation, we should consider what we say before just blurting out our thoughts. So it is, too, with martial arts training. While fighting, a degree of free-flowing thoughts and unconscious aptitude is required. During training, however, we need to remind ourselves of the basics, so our own form and interpretation don't drift off into another form of the original technique. This is not to say that karate techniques don't change over time. They certainly do. What is important is to honor the original lesson and form until such time as a new and improved form is created and adopted.

To honor our various roles in life, we should ask ourselves, "What don't I know?" periodically, to check in on how we can improve what we are doing and how we can evolve as a result.

###

Back in the Unimog, I reestablished the unconscious soldier's breathing, and he started to mumble. His eyes opened. He looked frightened.

I assured him he was going to be fine and that we were on our way back to camp. As my heart rate settled down, I realized that my actions over the last hour, while they had all been a reflection of the honor I had for my role as a platoon commander, they also honored my role as a human being. I thought about how my parents had raised me, and I was grateful to them for that. My mother was a nurse who always inspired me with her calm and caring manner, whenever my siblings or I would hurt ourselves. She didn't panic.

When the soldier fell off an obstacle course, he hit his head hard and had lost consciousness. The platoon looked to me, when we'd established that we didn't have a medic. I was probably not the most qualified, but I knew first aid, so I just got to work. I felt anxious, but I stepped through my anxiety. My job and my role in that job became more important than the ego-driven desire to avoid making a mistake.

Later that day, once the rest of the platoon had returned back to camp, we all trooped on down to the camp hospital to check in on the injured soldier. Everyone was in high spirits to see the soldier propped up in bed and looking well.

I told him he'd given me a bit of a scare. The soldier coughed to clear his throat, so the whole platoon could hear what he had to say.

He leaned forward, looked at me, and said, "Thanks for the kiss, sir."

We all had a good laugh at that. For the rest of the exercise, I was blown kisses at one time or another from pretty well everyone in the platoon. I thought about how strange a sign of honor can be.

1: Loyalty

*"I'm not in this world to live up to your expectations,
and you are not in this world to live up to mine."*

—Bruce Lee

My ears were ringing from the explosions that surrounded me. The Staff Sergeant was yelling at me. My eyes squinted, and I ducked my head, an involuntary response to another explosion on my right. I'd messed up a flanking maneuver and was now in the middle of a full-scale retreat. We were in open ground and completely exposed.

The Staff Sergeant was still yelling at me. "*Your comms are down*!" I looked behind me to see my radio man on the ground.

"Is he dead?" I asked.

"He may as well be. You need to get out of here."

I dropped to one knee and put down my Steyr AUG rifle. I grabbed my radio man's forearm and threw him onto my shoulder in a fireman's lift. I grabbed my rifle with my free hand and stood up. With adrenaline coursing through my veins, I gauged the weight on my shoulders and started the long walk toward cover.

The promised cover was just over a mile away.

So, what does a man who has been married (and divorced) twice have to say about loyalty?

I do not profess to offer marital advice, but the fact that I still laugh with and honor my two former wives is a testament to the respect we have for one another and the loyalty we have to the vows we made to always love each other. This book honors them both.

To be true to oneself is not always easy, but it is always essential. Loyalty is about a strong feeling of support or allegiance. Loyalty is about a commitment to love and honor something, but it does not necessarily mean living with someone or being legally married to them. Marriage can be a beautiful example of loyalty, but it does not define loyalty.

Without delving into the complexities of married life, I became more focused on being the "perfect husband" than being myself. The unfortunate insincerity of this stance (while quite honorable and with the best intentions) is to offer a shadow of oneself rather than the authentic happy samurai with his own mission and purpose. My heart was also closed off, as I mentioned in the chapter on courage.

I am not saying you cannot have a mission and purpose and still be happily married. I'm saying, without a defined mission and purpose that drives you, it is very difficult (if not impossible) to give yourself fully to loving your spouse/partner as your true, authentic self. Children (especially young children) pose a completely different challenge to married life, and loyalty to children should always trump all else. Loyalty and the associated responsibility parents have to bring up a child go above and beyond the loyalty between two people without children. I honor, respect, and admire parents who stick it out with the best intentions to provide for their children.

When you have a mission and a purpose, you can be a better friend, one who is there when the chips are down; you have the capacity to do so because of your sense of fulfillment. You can celebrate the joys of your friends' successes because you know what your personal mission is, and you can honor the myriad missions of other people in the same way. Loyalty is not a competition. It is being true to oneself, so we can be most authentic and present for others who are important to us.

I think of the example of politicians and senior corporate executives in this modern world we live in. Many members of a particular party/corporation will support a leader with whom they fundamentally disagree on ethical and/or moral issues. This is prevalent in every political party and large corporation in most countries. These disenchanted members of an organization still support the organization and are "loyal" to the organization. This is not loyalty in a bushido sense. This "loyalty" is appeasement at best and sycophantic or obsequious at worst. The fact is these loyal servants are not happy people. Their sense of alignment with their best selves is off kilter. The reward of power, prestige, or money is empty, vacuous, and unfulfilling.

The type of "loyalty" that is bound purely by money, guilt, or fear is poisonous to the soul. It makes us sad. The type of loyalty that is bound by love and compassion is rewarding and fulfilling and makes us happy. Loyalty starts and finishes with the heartfelt conscience of our best self.

In Kaicho's book, *The Human Face of Karate,* Kaicho talks about the joys and challenges of bringing Kyokushinkai karate to America. He also talks about the difficulty of his decision to resign from the Kyokushin Kaikan and open the Seido Juku school. This decision of conscience was in many ways heartbreaking for Kaicho, I'm sure, but his loyalty to karate and to teaching the "sincere way" was such that the decision had to be made. When we are driven by a passion for something that is real and genuine, we stay loyal to that authentic passion when we are able to recognize a change that makes that thing less genuine or a shadow of what it used to be in our hearts. That's not to say "quitting" is always the best option. But when the options have been exhausted in an attempt to rekindle what was once in our heart, we have a duty to our own conscience to make a decision.

The history of martial arts includes many stories of masters and students who have made a decision to go their own way or start a new style. The consciences of the individuals involved will have determined whether those moves were wise or not. We can agree or disagree with some of these decisions, but we should respect people's ability to follow their own path. We, too, have an obligation to be loyal to our own path. My path and my bushido "sincere way" is the study of Seido Karate-do, following Kaicho's example.

When (Shuseki Shihan) William Oliver decided to start his own style, Kenshikai Karate, I certainly did not agree with this decision, and I missed him but respected him. I still respect him all these years after his untimely death in 2004. Shuseki followed Kaicho when Seido Juku was founded, so his loyalty was always to Kaicho's teaching. I remain loyal to the memory of training with Shuseki, and I try to emulate some of the energy with which he taught. To discard those memories is to be disloyal to a beautiful and impactful part of my bushido training.

Loyalty to family is a powerful force and something I respect. In 2019, (Kancho) Ino Maquirang started Jin Sei Ryu Karate-do to establish a martial arts style for his family, among other things. (Kancho) Ino also followed Kaicho from Kyokushinkai karate to Seido, so his loyalty has been demonstrated over the years.

(Kancho) Ino was also a significant part of my early training at Seido and became a close friend. These conflicting loyalties can create a challenging situation. I look into my heart to remain loyal to the memories of what has created trust between us. I still feel a strong connection to and a unique martial arts allegiance with people whom I have had the privilege of training with over the years, despite the different uniforms we might wear.

The intention and motivation behind our loyalty are worth some reflection and serious examination. When we are drawn toward something that resonates with our best self and generates a feeling that we are connected with something in sync with our heart, we feel loyalty. When we are loyal to something we either don't trust or that makes us feel less than our best self, we feel a pressure to appease others, and this makes us sad. This is not loyalty but a form of entrapment.

We can unlearn what we have learned; we looked at this in the chapter on righteousness. As we evolve and understand more, we develop our wisdom, and we understand more based on the experience we've had. Unlike relearning (or unlearning) learned behaviors that we identify as not being in line with our best selves, we cannot "un-understand" things that we now understand in more detail. We can only understand something more as we seek the truth in things. Loyalty is like a commitment to a set of terms and conditions dictated by love and truth. If those terms and conditions change, then we must understand the new reality and assess our true loyalty as a result.

Loyalty begets loyalty. To create more loyalty in our lives, we must begin with our own loyalty to ourselves and then our own loyalty to others. Like respect, we cannot buy authentic loyalty from others. If we believe others are more loyal to us than we are loyal to them, we are fooling ourselves, because loyalty and trust do not work as a one-way phenomenon. We simply cannot ask someone else for the type of loyalty we are not willing to give them. To do so is assuming we are somehow "buying" them as a servant to our own needs. Such a relationship is not based on loyalty or love, but rather on obligation and authority. Even in a work environment, this type of quid pro quo has a limited shelf life when it comes to developing loyalty. It lacks honor.

The easiest way to test your own loyalty is to think about how you respond when people talk about your friends or family who are not present. Do you gossip about them behind their back or say negative things about them that you would not say to their face? Growing up, we have all been guilty of this, but there comes a time when we decide those days are over. That time is now. Stick up for those to whom you are loyal. Defend those who are not present. When we do this, without reward or recognition, we are being loyal to our own best self as well as to those we are loyal to. It feels good to be a loyal friend, and this gives us honor.

Sing praises about those people to whom you are loyal. Tell the world how special those people are in your life. Tell people how they earned your loyalty. The wealthiest people in the world are fascinated by this, because loyalty is one of the most valuable things we can experience in life. When we celebrate those to whom we're loyal, we help to spread the beauty of those wonderful souls, and we reaffirm that we are grateful and kindhearted.

When we say negative things about other people, we are recognized as someone who gossips, and our friends and family immediately suspect that we also gossip about them. Conversely, when we praise our friends and have kind words for them (behind their back), then we are recognized for the kind and generous happy samurai we are. Our friends and family are then more likely to be loyal to us, because they recognize us as worthy.

Think about the eulogy you would write for your best friend(s). Think about the type of eulogy you would like written about you. What is special and unique about that other person that makes them so important to you?

When you identify these things, share them through a kind word or a birthday card or a thank-you note.

When we are understood for who we are, we recognize loyalty and trust. The very character traits we would like to be recognized for are sometimes the traits we most need to acknowledge and recognize in those people closest to us. Through this recognition, those close to us are more likely to recognize the same in us. When we demonstrate a generous and loyal spirit, we attract like-minded people and generate loyalty.

Your vibe attracts your tribe, and your tribe reinforces your vibe. Another old expression, "Birds of a feather flock together," says the same thing. As we evolve and mature, we move forward and grow. The way we address the world allows us to engage with people who will fit into our future, in addition to those who have been part of our history. Through osmosis, we take on board the positive (and negative) attributes of the people we surround ourselves with. If we spend time with people who have an abundance mindset and feel grateful, we will think and feel the same. If we spend time with people who feel victimized and trapped, we will feel the same way. Our perspective of the world is reinforced by those we spend our lives with.

The world we experience reflects back our own intentions. Take a minute to close your eyes and think about three words in a eulogy that would encapsulate how you would like to be remembered by those closest to you. Those three words could be something like, "loving," "kind," "generous," or "bold." Whatever you feel best describes your unique gifts.

Write these words down. Think about these words each morning when you're in the shower (appreciating the warm water), and commit to doing something during the day that will demonstrate just one of those unique gifts. At the end of the day, think about these words and assess how they were reflected throughout the day.

The three words don't necessarily need to stay the same over time, so this is an ongoing process. You can repeat the exercise and identify three words at any time. What is most important to us changes over time, so this occasional reevaluation helps to ensure that our friendships are healthy and positive and we are remaining loyal to what is in our heart.

Once we establish a daily appreciation for three words that reflect what we consider to be our best self, we become more aware of others who demonstrate these traits. These people are our teachers and our strength. We still walk our own path, but we look to emulate the intention of these people and follow their example in our own way. We will be drawn toward the same energy that we transmit through our own actions and will be happier as a result. We become more self-aware as a consequence of becoming more tuned in and aware of the world around us.

Self-awareness will allow us to consider what makes us "tick" and how we can best be loyal to our authentic self. We all have flaws and faults, and we all have beauty and magnificence. Who are the like-minded people we want to share our life experiences with? When we are loyal to our own path, we allow these like-minded people to be drawn to us naturally, and our true intentions will naturally seek them out. Friendships and relationships always have challenges; loyalty, through honesty and trust, allows us to approach these challenges with an open, rather than defensive, closed heart. We cannot do any better than be our most genuine self, so there remains nothing else to "worry" about when we can be loyal to that beautiful human inside.

Give the world the best of you, and you will experience the best of the world. Like us, the world is not perfect, but it is a continual work in progress. We have a responsibility to be loyal to the effort required to give it our best shot. We never know whom we will influence through our actions and words. Teaching children is a big responsibility, because children often copy technique (and behavior) so accurately that a mistake in form (and behavior) will be replicated by the students in the class.

In the dojo and in the world, our behavior influences people in ways we cannot imagine. When we are trying to teach something specifically, it is often not the right time for the student to learn that particular lesson, so we cannot assume that the lessons we teach best are learned in the manner we anticipate.

Our example stands above all else. Talk is cheap when it is not backed up by action. To teach children to listen when we do not listen is simply a waste of breath. To teach karate students to try their hardest when we are coasting is just an empty ego trip. Hypocrisy is the polar opposite to the sincere way, so when we find ourselves teaching something that we are yet to learn (to the same level we expect of the students), we should take pause to consider teaching another lesson. Even when we are doing basic punching, we do ourselves proud when we just focus and give it our best effort. That's all we can do in this life—try our hardest and be proud of our ability to be loyal to that effort. We don't have to be expert at everything to provide the world an example of our best self. When people see our authentic best efforts, we are teaching the path of bushido, even when we are not aware of who we might be teaching.

It's all very well to demonstrate a fancy spinning back kick or a favorite kata, but the lesson is lacking if the intention is not correct. I think of the most impactful lessons I have learned over the years. They are all lessons taught to me through action(s) rather than words. Kaicho taught me always to pause before entering the dojo and to bow and say, "Osu," when we step onto the floor. I learned this from watching Kaicho. Nidaime taught me to stay focused when I'm teaching and to engage with every student in class. I learned this from watching Nidaime. (Sei Shihan) Paul Williams taught me to be calm and quiet before a tournament fight, because that is what he does, and I observed this. (Shuseki Shihan) Oliver taught me to stand still and stay silently focused when Kaicho is speaking. I learned this from watching him.

We touch the people we meet and leave an impression. When we take responsibility for this, we are more likely to conduct ourselves in a manner more in tune with who we are and what we're about.

We like to think we leave a positive impression with those we meet, but what are we doing to foster that? Think about those people in your life who observe you on a regular basis. What do you proactively do to create a positive impression for these people? When we are feeling grateful and loyal, we let go of the insecurities that make us "act" like somebody else, which allows us to simply be ourselves. Our natural state is to be more in tune with those around us; our behavior will reflect this, and we'll leave a positive impression as a result.

The Japanese word "Kizuna'" means to have bonds or connections to people. This is more than teamwork; it's more about interconnectedness. We need one another, and we should be grateful to others for forming the basis of our community. When people who share the same values work together, the result is bigger than the sum of the parts. This has nothing to do with politics or which school you went to or your favorite sports team. These types of "club" relationships can be "tribal" and meaningful (and fun), but they are not the same as Kizuna. Kizuna is a special bond that automatically garners loyalty because two people (or more) are instinctively on the same page and understand that they need one another to reach their potential. We need our fellow kohai in the dojo to reach our potential in martial arts training.

When we are loyal to our best self, we do not need to actively seek, or chase, people. Those people who share our values will naturally gravitate toward us. The loyalty and interconnectedness between people with the same love in their hearts is very simple and pure. The more we can tear away the ego and embrace our true authentic nature, the easier it is to communicate and connect with people, because we have nothing to hide.

We have nothing to prove. We have nobody to impress. We are just genuine and vulnerable (remember, that's the same as courageous), and the stress of living to someone else's ideals evaporates. We can't do any better than being our most authentic self.

Old friends are important and can prove to be a grounding influence. I have known some of my closest friends for forty years. You cannot be "fake" or fool these old friends, who know the very essence of what you're about. Loyalty to that history is a powerful force. We have a responsibility to check in on our circle of friends and the influence they have on us from time to time. Friends who are kind and compassionate will foster that energy in us. Friends who are bold and driven will help to develop that spirit in us. The world we perceive to be real is influenced heavily by those we choose to share our life with.

If we recognize a negative trait in those closest to us, we should examine our own behavior. If it's lust, victimization, shame, guilt, dependence, impatience, or anything that doesn't make us proud, we should consider what we are loyal to. We should look inward, not outward.

Someone with a gambling problem, for example, will surround themselves with gamblers, so the world is full of people who are rich or broke. We know this isn't the reality *we* live in, but it is the reality of someone with a gambling problem. An alcoholic will see only teetotalers and alcoholics in their world. A drug addict will be surrounded by drug users and, most likely, the police. It is not the "world's" issue but the individual's perspective. We must choose what we want to be loyal to.

We show loyalty to our best self when we create a habit of exercising our mind and our body every single day. Even if this consists of waking up and quickly doing ten pushups or ten squats or simply reading a passage out of a book. Why? Because we are worth the effort. Be good to yourself, so you can be your best for the world.

With a soldier slung over my shoulder and a mile to walk, I plodded through the tussock as dirt and debris rained down on me from the surrounding explosions.

The Staff Sergeant was still yelling at me. I'd blown my assignment. I was meant to lead a successful mission to capture a hill, and here I was retreating with only half of my platoon. I was carrying my radio operator with my metaphorical tail between my legs. A massive fail.

Battle simulation training is tough and exhausting and deliberately creates a "no-win" scenario to test your decision-making and your character under pressure. I was probably meant to leave my presumably dead radio operator, but something inside me wanted to prove that I was going to do something right among my many failures that day.

I thought about what I'd do in a real wartime situation under the same circumstances. We'll never know. I just knew I had to remain loyal to something. That determined mindset and sheer adrenaline helped me carry the soldier for more than a mile. I had no idea I was physically capable of doing that, and I was humbled by the power of loyalty.

1: Self-Control

"Courage is not the absence of fear, but the triumph over it."

—Nelson Mandela

The M67 fragmentation hand grenade was live and armed. It felt heavy in my hand. My palms were wet with sweat. The fuse would delay detonation by four to five seconds. I'd removed the safety pin, and the spring-loaded striker had been released.

I felt a little claustrophobic in the trench. I had enough room to bend my arm back to give the baseball-style grenade a decent throw. I'd thrown dummy grenades before, but this was my first live grenade. I steeled myself.

If you've read this far, I'll let you in on a little secret. Being a happy samurai in the twenty-first century starts and ends with self-control. While each chapter of this book has listed one of the eight tenets of the Samurai as equally important to the others, they all require a degree of self-control. It is therefore fitting that self-control is the last chapter of this book. Self-control is a daily battle between the mind and the body. There's no way around it. We all have to face it, whether we like it or not, so we might as well face it head on and get on with it. We have to replace fear with love.

We all fear change. It's the unknown. Self-control requires a change to learned behaviors that motivate us to continue doing the same things. If we do this over many years, we end up living more in the past (living with regret) or in the future (living with anxiety), instead of live in the present. Self-control requires us to do battle with our own ego. The bridge between goals and accomplishments is self-discipline. Nothing else makes the cut, despite the myriad excuses and rationalizations our ego makes in defense of a lack of self-control.

How does our ego relate to the tenets of the Samurai? Our ego thinks we have it all sorted out and can find justification for ignoring our instincts, when we know we're doing something that is not righteous or true. Our ego will tell us not to be vulnerable or courageous and to "save face," instead of risking being "seen" as our true self.

Our ego will tell us that benevolence is for suckers, and we're better off hording whatever we can for our own gratification. Our ego will tell us that respect shows weakness and will escalate our own insecurities to justify this. Our ego might tell us we need to lie and cheat and be insincere, if we are to get what we want. Our ego will actually tell us we don't deserve to love ourselves (which sounds ridiculous), because we are less than we should be or what we "deserve" to be; it will cast us as a victim in the world.

Our ego will let us off the hook, if we are inconsistent with our ethics and integrity. Our ego will, of course, conclude that self-control (gaining command over the ego) is a dumb idea, so why even try to do battle with the great, all-powerful, mighty ego?

Our ego is a cynical bully over our best self.

This is the bit you might not want to hear. To gain command over the ego, we need to meditate. Meditation is like doing jiu-jitsu (literally grappling) with your ego. Kaicho instructs all of his students to meditate every day, even if it's for a minute. It took me many years to appreciate the value of this, and I did not regularly meditate for a large portion of my life as a martial artist.

Kaicho also encouraged me to compete in tournaments but cautioned me to not focus too much on this aspect of my training. I have competed and won tournaments in kumite and kata in Jamaica, New Zealand, Australia, Italy, and throughout the USA, and while this validated hard training and dedication (which is good), it did not bring a better command or control of my ego. In fact, tournament "success" often brought about even less control of my ego.

Meditation delivers direct benefits immediately. Even if you take a minute to sit still in the morning, you'll approach the day with just a little more clarity than if you stumbled out of bed and just went directly into your normal routine. If you take a minute to sit still and appreciate your day before you go to sleep, you'll be more at ease when your head hits the pillow. The longer you meditate and the more consistently you meditate, the greater the benefits. It's as simple as that. Meditation is like taking your mind to the gym.

As I'm writing this, my ego (and, most likely, yours as well) is saying, "Hang on! I don't live in a cave. I can't check out of the world and meditate all day!" This is true. I currently aim to meditate for twenty minutes each morning and twenty minutes each night. Sometimes I settle for ten minutes.

The discipline to take responsibility for self-control (which sounds like an oxymoron) is to do something to exercise control of the mind every day. Some people meditate for thirty minutes each morning. I find that hard to do every day. Start with just thirty seconds. Like brushing your teeth, think about leaving the house with a "cleaner/quieter" mind, and make this a habit. Before you go to bed, find that small pocket of time to just do some jiu-jitsu with your ego. This is the path of self-control.

Is it easy to meditate every day? No, it's not easy. Most things of value do not come easily, but they are worth the effort. Does mediation get a little bit easier over time? Yes, it does. I still have days when my mind is full of activity and chaos and I don't feel like meditating. I have days when I don't feel like training, but once I start, I'm always so glad I did. The same is true of meditation. I can guarantee you'll never finish a meditation and think that you shouldn't have done it. Meditation will make it easier for you to be happy.

Meditation will not allow you to figure out or fully understand the motivations of other people, but it will absolutely allow you to figure out and understand your own motivations in more depth. Your sense of self-awareness is dramatically enhanced with consistent meditation. As Aristotle said, "We are what we repeatedly do. Excellence, therefore is not an action but a habit." Our challenge is to develop good habits and eliminate bad habits through discipline and self-control.

In Stephen Covey's famous book, *The Seven Habits of Highly Effective People*, he talks about sharpening the saw. Rather than keep sawing away with a blunt saw, take time out to sharpen the saw, so you'll be more effective and efficient as a result. Even our best efforts with a blunt saw fall way short of our efforts with a sharp saw.

I read Covey's book in my early twenties, and it had a profound impact on my approach to karate training. But I hadn't considered meditation or self-control as part of that. When we meditate, we literally take the mind away from the daily grind of sawing, and we sharpen the edge so we can use our mind more efficiently and effectively. We make the mind stronger. When we meditate, we simply spend time with ourselves to reenergize the mind.

Discipline actually frees us from the shackles of previous bad habits, so we become empowered to make more, and better, decisions. Like weightlifting or swimming, the more we practice self-control (big or small) and the more frequently we practice self-control, the more confidence we gain in our ability to execute self-control when needed. Even when we slip up and go back to a "bad habit," there's no need to give up and feel despondent.

Our challenge is to recognize when we're lacking self-control and manage the situation with some of the techniques we've discussed in earlier chapters. Remember Gassho. When you place your palms together, fingers pointing up, you can pause (even for a few seconds) and practice what I like to think of as a "mini meditation" to calm the mind. When we control the body and breathing, we can wrestle with the mind.

Don't expect a dramatic ascension into bliss or a profound enlightenment, when you start meditating. It doesn't quite work like that. I wish it did! It's a process of getting stronger, day by day. Think of the change you'd see in your physical body after a year of yoga or running three times a week. The change in your mind and your perspective strengthens in the same way with meditation. Like training at the dojo, consistency will redound to benefits and rewards. Consistent meditation builds strength upon strength and calms the mind as it gets stronger. Einstein said, "No problem can be solved from the same level of consciousness that created it." Meditation allows us to reach a different (higher) level of consciousness and awareness, so we can better tackle problems.

We should not be impatient with our training or with meditation. Remember that "Do" means "way," rather than destination. We walk a path rather than take a freeway. Kaicho talks about "Renma chikuseki," which means, "Keep polishing—accumulate." As we train and walk the path, we develop and accumulate. We build on our training to be more centered, more balanced, more grounded. We seek the perfection of technique while acknowledging we will never be "perfect" at karate; we will be, however, that hardworking student who keeps polishing. Self-control will allow us to accumulate knowledge and understanding far beyond technique.

Technique, on its own, still takes patience and perseverance. The three most basic building blocks of karate take three years (each) to "master" to a level of competence.

"Nigiri" means "fist." To make a fist properly takes three years.

"Tachi" means "stance." To stand in a balanced stance correctly takes three years.

"Tsuki" means "strike." To strike correctly and consistently takes three years.

It takes at least three years of dedicated training to acquire each of these basic karate-do skills. Patience is an essential element at this stage of training. Like life, "Do" (way) is an ongoing journey.

As karate students, we reassess these basic techniques and revisit them when executing, for example, a basic punch. We make a proper fist, stand balanced, and strike with the first two knuckles (Seiken). Injuries will create obstacles to maintaining a balanced stance, so we sometimes need to relearn what we have learned. After hip surgery, I needed to relearn my proper, balanced stance from scratch. This is karate-do training.

We say, "Osu," many times at the dojo. "Osu" is short for "Oshi Shinobu," which means many things, including, "I will continue to try my best." You cannot do any better than trying your best.

Self-control will manifest into your life if you simply continue to try your hardest. Think of somebody you love and care about, and consider how you would "coach" that person to become the best they can possibly be. Think about how you would compliment them and congratulate them on their achievements. Think about what discipline would help keep them on track and away from negative influences. Now apply all of that to yourself. Say, "Osu," and face the day like a champion.

Obedience implies compliance to a set of rules or laws that are established through someone else's external authority. Think of self-control as obedience to the laws you set for yourself. You have complete control over how you choose to live your life, and you alone determine what is important to you. Nobody else can define what is important to you and what will make you happy. No governing body can decide what you choose to give to the world as your unique gift. When you define those character traits you feel best represent what you are most proud of (and who you want to be), you write your own laws that you obey. You have the power to walk your path.

Righteousness takes self-control. We have the ability to set out on a path of righteousness, regardless of the road we have already travelled. Meditation will create more insight into what we know to be righteous and will empower us to make better choices when required to do so. We will still slip up from time to time, and when we do, we need to get back on the path and feel confident in our own ability to try our very hardest to be righteous.

To be righteous requires us to test our command over our ego and proactively work toward being our best self, without the need for reward or recognition. When we do the right thing despite not being seen, we build on our integrity and become stronger. We also become happier when we know who we are and we become prouder of that person. When we are righteous to ourselves, we will become more righteous to the world.

Courage takes self-control. Facing our fears and coming to terms with those fears takes courage. We need to be vulnerable to be able to address those things that scare us most. This is our greatest measure of courage. Knowing we can face these fears and not shy away from them develops more courage in our mind, body, and spirit.

Fear can be very real and functional; but, more often than not, fear is a figment of our imagination. When we reduce fear to the place it belongs (which is not in the "real" here and now, but only in our mind), we become happier as a result and gain perspective on our present reality, rather than the false reality that our fears will have us believe. The happy samurai will always face down fear, because love is always stronger than fear. Self-love and self-respect will make us more courageous.

Meditation, like physical training, is good for us. When we are good to ourselves, we create abundance in our hearts and the ability to share that with others. Benevolence makes us feel free, because we cannot feel like victims when we are giving with a kind heart. Empathy and compassion destroy our feelings of unworthiness and victimization and replace them with tranquility and peace. We are not at war with the world when we are compassionate toward it. To be happier, feel grateful for what you have, and share from that place. What we want most is the very thing we all need to give more of.

To develop respect for others, we need to respect ourselves first and foremost. Self-control allows us to respect ourselves and feel happy we are living lives that are true and authentic. While we respect people most for being genuine and real, the same can be said for attracting respect from others. While it is an honor to be respected, the only thing we can really control is the respect we have for, and show, others. Respect is something we give rather than something we get. When we search for ways to become more respectful, we automatically become more present and more "in tune" with the world. When we are more present, we see more and experience more and have many more reasons to smile, appreciate, and be happy.

Sincerity requires a certain degree of self-control and requires us to take a pause when we're on the cusp of gossiping or needlessly exaggerating or downright lying. Meditation will enhance our self-awareness and allow us to recognize that our authentic self is a thing of incredibly unique beauty. We do not serve ourselves well when we play the part in someone else's play or drama. We can only be our best if we are true to ourselves, and this is something to treasure. We become more and more sincere little by little, day by day. We cannot be (or become) anyone else other than our sincere selves. The world does better when you turn up and deliver your unique gifts, because you'll be truly happier and far more original.

Honor is learned but needs to be practiced. When we are proactive about being honorable, we create a world of meaning and purpose. One of greatest gifts we can give to those we love is to honor them with the gift of trust. It takes discipline to improve our ability to listen more deeply to what others say; we honor people when we pay close attention. As we develop a better and more intimate appreciation for people in our lives, we will be "in sync" and in a far more natural rhythm with them. When we are determined to understand before being understood, we develop an incredible amount of empathy, and we honor those people whom we seek to appreciate and know more deeply. We will continue to be delighted with the insights we gain.

Loyalty to our best self takes self-control and discipline. We are blessed with a mind, a body, and a spirit to look after and develop. We are the stewards and custodians of our own lives. We are far more capable of being loyal to those we love when we are loyal to our own set of virtues and values. When we read more, we appreciate we are not alone, and we learn to view the world from multiple perspectives. It's useful to read or study something every day. When we exercise, we create energy and improve our mental health as well as reduce our risk of many diseases. It's important to do some sort of exercise every day. When we exercise our spirit, we become more grounded and self-aware and happy. We owe it to ourselves to meditate every day.

Far from the calm of meditation, I threw the hand grenade about twenty metres from the trench and ducked down to brace for the concussive explosion. After a beat, I heard the muffled detonation. I shuffled out of the trench and made way for the next person in line. Self-control had allowed me to embrace the test and move forward.

Conclusion

L ife is full of strange lessons that test your ability to be present in the moment. I have learned over the years that I don't need to be in a hand grenade range trench or flying a shaking Strikemaster to appreciate the value of being in the here-and-now. It's still a challenge to be present, but it gets a little easier with practice.

Please continue to consider the eight tenets and discover how to apply them to every-day life.

* Righteousness

* Courage

* Benevolence

* Respect

* Sincerity

* Honor

* Loyalty

* Self-Control

My hope is, through the examination of these tenets of the samurai, we can face our fears and make the choice to live the life of our dreams rather than the life of our fears. Many of those fears are dictated to us by our history. We cannot rewrite our history or change where we have come from, but we can write the rest of the story from where we are right now.

There is no other place to start the new journey than here and now. Today is your day and now is your time to live in the moment and move forward. You and you alone can control your ability to be happy. You and you alone can control how you wish to relate to this beautiful world we live in.

I'd like to express my heartfelt gratitude to you, for reading my book. If you place your palms together in "Gassho" and close your eyes, I hope you feel the appreciation I have for you, as I sit at my desk and write the final sentence of this book. That is my gift to you, from one Happy Samurai to another.

Osu.

Acknowledgements

All of the military experiences I have shared in this book are true and accurate. It is important to note, however, that none of my experiences happened in the theatre of war. I can only imagine how hard it is for combat soldiers to share their wartime experiences. What I have shared took a certain degree of vulnerability, but it is a trifle compared to the vulnerability required by soldiers who have endured the trauma of war. I honor those veterans who live with the harsh and brutal memories of war.

My love and respect to all whom I have had the honor to train with over the years. To name a few:

Kaicho, Nidaime, Hanshi Charles Martin, Hanshi Andy Barber, Hanshi Renzie Hanham, Kancho Jack Sims Sensei, Shihan Neil Parker, Terry Daniels Sensei, Mrs Smith, Wayne Smith, Shihan Anthony Netzler, Professor John Danaher, Dan Willman, Shihan William Oliver, Sei Shihan Gil Alstein, Shuseki Shihan William Best, Shuseki

Shihan Christopher Caile, Shuseki Shihan Eli Bitran, Sei Shihan Judy Curiale, Sei Shihan Michelle Cuttino, Sei Shihan Nancy Lanoue, Sei Shihan Sarah Ludden, Sei Shihan John "Ace" McGettigan, Sensei Scott Wilson, Sei Shihan Matthew Warshaw, Sei Shihan Billy Macagnone, Sei Shihan Vincent Macagnone, Sei Shihan Dwayne Roberts, Sei Shihan Pam Roberts, Kyoshi Leighton Roberts, Sensei Albie Mitchell, Paul Basin, Sensei Roxanne Blatz, Sei Shihan Toshihide Sawahira, Sei Shihan Masaru Inden, Senpai Watanabe, Kyoshi Nelson Young, Kyoshi Susie Marples, Kyoshi Mike Schwartz, Senpai Meg Nakamura, Kaori Hagi Nakamura, Hakim Walker, Jun Shihan Chris Sinclair, Shihan David Washington, Senpai Greg Burton, Jimmy Shanahan, Sensei Pat Brown, Kyoshi Hagai Bitran, Sei Shihan Ben Otang, Jun Shihan Scott Holdsworth, Jun Shihan Patrick Holden, Jun Shihan Eric Hughes, Kyoshi Fiona Fulton, Darrell Dodds, Kyoshi Troy Ballantyne, Patu Noble, Violet Zaki, Jun Shihan Kim Sawers, Shihan Leigh Maquirang, Shihan Sean Beehan, Senpai Max Maquirang, Sensei Maya Valeria, Lisa Morris, Sensei Don Cherry, Sensei Rudy Coppin, Sensei Michael Lorenz, PJ Valentini, Joey Docil, Michael & Maria Greenfield, Sensei Angel Alicea, Jun Shihan Karen Fisher, Kyoshi Daniel Tierney, Kyoshi Barbara Rothenberg, Kyoshi Monica Harris, Senpai Joel Forman, Senpai Yukie Sugahara, Kyoshi Barry Williams, Bernie Petty, Jun

Shihan Ted Pastrick, Shihan Teri McDuffie, Sensei Jack Sabat, Jason Pichardo, Dr. Izzy Lira, and so many more.

I would also like to thank the following people who helped me on this journey with their encouragement, instruction, and feedback. Nothing we do is self-made. We all learn from somebody.

Daphne Mayes (my mother), Jun Shihan Phillip Tomlinson, Kyoshi Bekah Fisk, Kancho Ino Maquirang, Jay Roston, Jun Shihan Meredith Sawers Pretto, Sei Shihan Paul Williams, and Sei Shihan Debra Hershkowitz (editor extraordinaire) were the first people to read my drafts. My heartfelt gratitude goes out to you all.

About the Author

Luke Mayes has studied karate for over forty years and worked at the House of Dormeuil for nearly thirty years. Born in England and raised in New Zealand, Luke went to Rosmini College and is a graduate of Auckland University. Luke served in the Royal New Zealand Air Force as a pilot and also served in the Royal New Zealand Army as an Officer in the Territorial Force.

A fifth-degree black belt at Seido Karate, (Kyoshi) Luke has been teaching karate for over twenty-five years. Luke spent twenty years in New York City and continues to study at the School of Practical Philosophy. He now lives in California, where he teaches Seido Karate while providing self-defense training at the Jody House Brain Injury Support Center and at the Braille Institute Santa Barbara.

Made in the USA
Columbia, SC
18 May 2021